T0063262

Jar Full of Change

WITH A DASH OF LOVE

Nancy Dybek Greene

authorHOUSE®

AuthorHouse™
1663 Liberty Drive
Bloomington, IN 47403
www.authorhouse.com
Phone: 1-800-839-8640

© 2015 Nancy Dybek Greene. All rights reserved.

No part of this book may be reproduced, stored in a retrieval system, or
transmitted by any means without the written permission of the author.

Published by AuthorHouse 09/23/2015

ISBN: 978-1-4969-5264-6 (sc)
ISBN: 978-1-4969-5263-9 (e)

Print information available on the last page.

Any people depicted in stock imagery provided by Thinkstock are models,
and such images are being used for illustrative purposes only.
Certain stock imagery © Thinkstock.

This book is printed on acid-free paper.

Because of the dynamic nature of the Internet, any web addresses or links contained in
this book may have changed since publication and may no longer be valid. The views
expressed in this work are solely those of the author and do not necessarily reflect the
views of the publisher, and the publisher hereby disclaims any responsibility for them.

Contents

PROLOGUE

How many creative, mouth-watering and savory decisions have been made out of the amount of change in a jar? Especially, the necessity of what's for dinner?

My Mother's change jar was a deep-blue Swedish commemorative coffee jar. It was labeled "Var So Gut" across the face among red and Swedish blue flowers and Nordic greenery. On the back it read Wilkommen.

Her Mother's (my Grandmother's) change jar was a teapot from a town near Krakow where she was born. Mine, is a beautiful lavender, square glass matchbook container from France given to me by my boss Lorraine, the owner of a restaurant named French Kitchen, where I worked with my then, teenage daughter.

In Peru, Indiana, where my daughter was born, the change jar on my sunny yellow kitchen window sill, was an Airforce "tin beer mug" from the base commissary that read USAF on the face of it, in blue lettering across the metal gray tin mug. My husband brought it home from the base plumbing shop where he worked on a Sac Air Force bomber base. His Sergeant Boss brought in beers for his birthday. He poured the frothy "Black Label" yellow, Indiana brew, into the shining tin "plumbing shop" US Flag decorated steins.

My daughter had been a "Preemie". In those days at six months old, she went to sleep at 6 PM for the night. So, I left my husband and baby to baby sit local children next door for a few hours while my neighbor drove her turquoise and white finned 55 Chevy to Wabash to her night waitress job.

I would watch her four children during this gap, until her husband came home from his full time job in construction. Sometimes I would finish her dinner preparations. Always, she would pay me from her tip money the next day over the fence in the back yard, often supplemented, if short on tip money from her shift, with a few vegetables from her garden.

Just as in the past I had done my Mother's grocery shopping from her tip jar filled with change and singles, she had made at the Swedish Club, my neighbor relied on her tips sometimes during those late week, grocery needy days. When shopping for my Mother, the fifty cents she gave me, for a 12 year olds choice of a pound of hamburger, liver or halibut left me coming back usually, with hamburger or halibut. Her beautiful blue vase "change jar" was the one she received from the Club the night the King and Queen of Norway visited. She tapped the change out of the special jar meagerly as I envisioned what I would really buy. In those days, my Mother often ran out of groceries close to Thursday. So Thursday dinner could be very challenging.

On Friday my Uncle Tony delivered the groceries. He delivered them from the grocery store he owned with his wife, my Aunt Elsie, my Mother's Sister. As kids growing up, we were happy to smell his cigar smoke in our second floor hallway late on a Friday afternoon. It elicited the hunger pains for ice cream, honey wafers, sugar syrup to mix what we called cool aid in those days, and chocolate milk. To this day, the pungent odor of a cigar brings happy feelings to my psyche mixed with hunger pains to my palate and stomach.

Later, as a young Mother of an infant, I found one could greatly benefit by keeping the traditional family change jar. After a while, as a young college student-mother, with a life of waitressing, home-making and studying; happiness could often be a hand full of change to run out for some fresh lemon or anchovies to complete a gourmand dish.

Change in a jar is exacting, demanding boundaries for creativity and planning ahead for an awareness of seasonal foods. (It has also paid many a milk money bill at school or bought an unexpected trip for my daughter to the candy or ice cream parlor.)

In these days of my credit/debit card having become my life; I am still delighted when I pull the box of matches out of my beat up French jar with the purple and yellow solitary iris etched into the front glass; only to find; that even in these days of our "empty nester" reversion to a honeymoon-like life; that coins have actually again been dispatched to the bottom, under the matches, out of the magic of an old subconscious habit!

Happy Cooking it says to my searching fingers!

CHAPTER ONE

DELICIOUS MEAL PLANNING

OF COURSE, in order to use a jar full of change effectively, there is a great deal of planning in shopping and storing quantities of ingredients through the year that will enhance the use of a "change jar" dinner decision. Sometimes, even a "little" gardening goes a long way.

AND OF COURSE, the only real reason to cook, is to eat. And the only real reason to eat is not only to be fit for life, but the visceral and aesthetic "real something" to look forward to everyday. My Father used to accuse my Mother of "Living to Eat" while he "Ate (only) to live". This describes simply to me the heights and depths of the participation in the joy of Food. But, a passion for food, does not always mean that one will also eat well. My Mother consumed a cake she baked almost everyday because she loved sweets. Also it was her delight to imitate the exotic petite fours she served at the country club. Her pantry was always well stocked with Cream of Tartar, Baking Flour, Powder Sugar and Brown Sugar, Karo Syrup and other necessary baking ingredients that I never witnessed in the homes of some of my childhood friends. Still, this made me aware of the difference sometimes, in the values of families when it came to home made food or TV dinners. It gave me a value of how my Mother's desserts were special creations she had duplicated from the Nordic chefs of the world, whereas my friends were lucky to get a "Twinkie" or "Hostess Muffin" for a desert from our corner candy store. And, all from a jar full of change!

Unlike my Mother, I have always been a "meat and potatoes" girl. Meals I later experienced in life, also in a restaurant like my Mother were Hungarian Goulash and Chicken Paprikash and Pepper Steak! So my jar of change was geared for a different venue in eating which included my dieting ethic and gardening techniques for more wholesome and deliciously fresh meals!

Using the same dictates for "simple but good" as my Grandmother and Mother did, I evolved my own gourmet style with the use of an eye on thrift and use of a seasonal garden to the max that I was able. Meals, based on what is fresh and available. Also very important, is to keep a well stocked larder. Flour, rice, condiments, spices, certain canned staples and flavorings and baking ingredients are all vital to have on hand to take full advantage of cooking for health while keeping expenses down.

II.

Once a month I do a grocery shopping that includes a list of all of the above to restock what I have used from my larder in the month that has passed. I replace often used items like tomato sauce, paste, canned mushrooms that are used often in lieu of fresh ones being on sale. Flour, vegetable oil, sugar, powdered and brown, rice, instant and regular, instant mashed potatoes and chili powders and taco mixes, canned beans, kidney and black are always on this list.

Creamed canned soups or tomato soups used for cooking and sauces can also be gotten at these types of stores for well less than one third of the price than our most popular Super Markets. They are essential for quick, no work sauces. There are items I use for cooking like canned spinach, peas, veg-all types of mixes and certain canned fruits for baking or glazes (like canned peaches or apricots) that I added to as needed in my stockpile. Also evaporated milk and dry milk packets that can be used in a pinch or in baking after they are doctored up a little with buttermilk, or the use of a little lemon juice.

These items are invaluable when it comes to making a quick coffee bread out of a store's own brand of "Bisquick" mix that is ready on a shelf. Treats like this and the smell in the house on an otherwise dreary day keep one busy using the oven for warmth and pleasant odors for appetites and some pleasures while being stuck indoors.

Spices get added to my stock-pile when on sale once or twice a year (usually in January after the holidays)) or right from the Garden, after drying them and using containers I've saved from other things to store and label them. Things like extracts for baking and baking powder or soda are usually never on sale, so I buy them only at the most trendy generic type stores where you do your own bagging, etc. In these stores, I can buy baking goods for one third of the price that they sell for in popular expensive supermarkets. One must always end up for one thing or another in a full service supermarket that can't be found in the generic or Hispanic stores like decaffeinated teas, and baking items such as currants, raisins, cranberries, and nuts. Ethnic stores, while diverse in spices for it's own ethnic group are limited in regular baking goods or gourmet coffees or teas or pet food selection.

But these same ethnic stores are the place to stock up on meat and poultry to keep a well diversified freezer at the lowest possible price. A freezer inexpensively stocked with various meat items can add to the joy of cooking nutritional meals often at the touch of opening a freezer door to find sale pot roast cut up by myself and ready for Hungarian Goulash.

III.

So, staples are put on a running list near my phone and I purchase them all year long on a monthly basis. This, is the basis for savings. But, the real savings comes in with the weekly sale papers for fresh vegetables, fruit and meats. These are what I stock my freezer with in the way of meat and Chicken in order to make the most nutritious meals with the least amount of expense.

$10 a week is all it really takes to keep a well—stocked and varied meats and poultry freezer full cheaply. When chicken is 39 cents a pound for leg quarters I buy all that will fit in my freezer from that sale week. If whole chickens are on sale the next week, (sometimes as low as 59 cents a pound) I fill the freezer again. If it's loin end pork chops for anywhere in my Hispanic markets from 69 cents to 99 cents a pound I spend a weekly amount of no more than $10.00. When half your freezer is already full, this amount is all it takes weekly to add interest to future meals.

If I can purchase hamburger at a certain Greek butcher shop for 99 cents a pound, I will buy ten pounds. I form it into one pound chunks for spaghetti sauces or tacos and single patties for my husband to devour by himself on a night when I cannot be home for dinner. Also, I watch this store for sales on lamb shoulder or ground lamb. Lately, I have been hard fixed to find Lamb Shanks anywhere and when I have, they are really expensive. Once, I was able to get a package of frozen ones with a coupon at Cosco, a Club member-ship type store, even with the coupon they were about 12.00 for the package of 3. I chalked this up to it being a treat!

There is also another thing I have always done to keep life interesting inexpensively by utilizing my plain old top of the refrigerator freezer to the max. I keep frozen "cool whip" for pie or sundae toppings, so that it can be ready. Also I keep the most generic chocolate, butterscotch and strawberry sauces for sundaes in the "fridge" on a shelf designated for just this category with containers of nuts that I have chopped from larger quantities and put in small containers for that shelf. In this way, they are always there to compliment a dessert and when the container is empty it goes right onto the list or I take my large nut cache out and refill the container with freshly chopped nuts.

When my daughter was still at home she always knew these items could be found quickly if she wanted a snack in the evening and no one was around to chop nuts, or make Sunday toppings like the hot fudge she just heated straight from inexpensive refrigerated chocolate sauce.

IV.

There is yet another component to using a freezer well. Whenever I make a roast, or roast more than one chicken, I put a few pieces of the meat away (if it is not going too fast). In this way, I have something I can make into a sandwich or add to another dish like a topping for a soup or to make a meat pot pie.

Many quick and delicious chicken or turkey salad can be made in minutes from scraps freshly frozen or a chicken chow mien with these frozen morsels of meat, a frozen green pepper that I cored and stored and a can of Chinese vegetables from my larder or just a can of bean sprouts. (I buy colored bell peppers when they are on sale, sometimes 10 cent sales, and core them. I put the tops in one plastic freezer bag for omelets and other uses and the pepper cups in another clear bag, all cored and cleaned and frozen so I can see what I have through the transparent bags I save from buying vegetables in the store.) Frozen Pork, Beef, or Turkey that's already cooked can be used in the same way or in other recipes such as Pepper Steak, etc.

In years past, when chickens still came with gizzards and livers inside, I would separate these into separate plastic bags and when I had enough of livers I would make chicken liver pate for an appetizer for company. With the gizzards I would make a delicious sautéed gizzard and onion dish and pour it over rice. Sometimes I would wrap the well cooked, tender gizzards with bacon and serve them as an appetizer also. Now, I am forced to buy chicken livers for pate, but I notice that I have never bought gizzards separately for anything.

Fruits, vegetables and packages of pasta or noodles, can be found on sale weekly at the Hispanic stores in my neighborhood. These wonderful fresh grocers have fresh Spinach or Romaine often for 69 cents a bunch, asparagus for 79 to 99 cents a bunch and cucumbers and green onions 4 for $1.00. Lemons and limes can go from 4 for $1 to 10 for $1. When you have a well stocked larder, and meat in your freezer, this is where the change in the jar comes in handy for fresh fruits and vegetables, like

$1 dollar pineapples or 10 cent apples and oranges. As long as I live near these stores, I can get my pasta for 4 packages for $1.00 and never higher than 3 packages for $1.00. These are mix and match and I can buy 3 to 4 packages of soup noodles or different pastas, like shell, orzo, alphabet noodles or plain spaghetti at almost any time. These packages of pasta can last me for a few months.

In the chapters ahead, I will share recipes and more wonderful secrets of 40 years of cooking very inexpensively and deliciously often with only the change in a jar. Added, is a special garden section with delicious almost no cost dishes all summer and fall. Also, my Lenten chapter has many dishes that cost less than $1.00 per day, per family. Though many of these dishes are Ethnic, I have picked only those that are healthy and really dishes people go to Ethnic stores to get, spending big money just to impress company with a few interesting side dishes.

V.

With today's days of a prolonged recession, many of these foods have been re-incorporated into the diets of many, remembering dishes they might have eaten in childhood, fed to them by their parents and Grandparents, only to perhaps resort back to their wonderful flavors and maybe without as much fat.

If you have found yourself lately with more time on your hands than money, you will love my little cookbook! Shopping is key and taking the time in markets and being aware of what markets consistently make the best nutritious foods available at next to nothing prices, can start a whole new life trend enjoying your leisure time creating things you love to eat while saving yourself some cash.

CHAPTER TWO

THE COLOR OF DINING ADVENTURES

The adventure? How little can you spend and how healthy an adventure can you make in one meal, at one time? How much color and variety and flavor?

AND OF COURSE, to the utmost of enjoyment. Biting into the pleasure of something really delicious can seem like a holiday to another world and culture. These everyday events, like three squares a day, are opportunities to create two or three experiences to look forward to in an otherwise busy or humdrum work day life.

Growing up in a Polish and Czech neighborhood in the big city and in the vicinage where we now live, eating at Food Counters and little ethnic restaurants can give one this experience everyday. With each meal I make, I try to do this at home. All of this is based on what is fresh and available and dirt cheap (a pun on garden fare); and which stores put out weekly flyers that have some consistency of food items that are desirable like Whole Chicken and Fresh Fish and Cuts of Meat that you use most in cooking. In a community where there is competition for business between little markets, one's grocery budget can really thrive.

In the inner city neighborhood where we live, the Hispanic stores get competition from the Polish stores, and our Jewel tries to keep up with all of this. It is good for getting good prices as well as real deals as specialty food items. For instance, Polish people eat creamed herring on the holiday and I cannot believe when I find a whole 16 oz. Jar for $6.00. This is what ethnic food competition does for the alert buyer. The Hispanic stores offer spices that Jewel has priced very high, sometimes by different names and only packaged in plastic bags, rather than glass or traditional tin spice containers. It makes shopping interesting and colorful.

Having baking staples on hand for whipping up a trip to the Scottish Highlands, via a cooking whim and a platter of scones, can happen in your own kitchen every day. Punctuated with delights such as a few fresh blueberries from a local sale can make summer, a little present, in the middle of winter. I usually have to make scones with staples such as currants or raisins from my baking cupboard. This, can turn an otherwise dismal and somber winter afternoon into a midday High Tea in the British Isles.

I am a list person . . . . I guess you could say that lists are the organization of all things big and small, preparations for activities, meal creations, vacation planning's and bill paying. Without a list for everything, even only a small mental list or plan for a span of a few months, I would be "listless". Lists are the vital device enabling you to check on yourself to see if life is going the way you planned. They can also make sure life IS GOING to go the way you plan it, short and long range. Lists are also the brain reliever of those whose ideas come too fast and often, the aid of an aging memory track overwhelmed by a new store, and a mapped plan for the "Morrow" that relieves the mind for sleep at night. Lists can be designed to save money, time and often add to the enjoyment of future endeavors like planning a vacation.

This list is one that hung on an apple decorated cork bulletin board I bought for a quarter in a garage sale. It hung on the kitchen cabinet next to my wall phone. In those years it was handwritten and had baking dough and shortening on it from trying to write on it with sticky baker's hands and (the hole in my inventory)record what was used; and needed to be bought again as I went along. Now I print this list out from my computer with enough squares behind each item for 6 months, to check off replacements while cooking. At the bottom, there is a place for notes about buying the item from the weekly neighborhood sale flyers. (Sometimes these items are featured more cheaply on a weekly basis in Ethnic stores than in the generic stores where I do my monthly shopping).

THESE ARE STAPLES I ALWAYS NEED:

FLOUR	MAYONNAISE
SUGAR	VINEGAR
BISQUICK TYPE MIX (ANY BRAND)	
POWDERED SUGAR	PICKLES (ANY DILL)
BROWN SUGAR	KETCHUP
RICE (Brown, Regular & Instant)	MUSTARD
VEGETABLE OIL	HOT SAUCE (3 FOR $1.00) WILL
BULK NUTS or GRAPE NUTS CEREAL	
BAKING SODA & POWDER	
SHORTENING I	INSTANT MASHED POTATOES
CORN MEAL OR MIX (JIFFY)	SALE CAKE MIXES (1-2)
RAISINS BOXED	COOKED DRIED BACON (1 PKG)
1 SACK DRY BEANS (ANY KIND,BUT PREFERABLY NAVY)	

CANNED GOODS:

TUNA – 2-3 CANS   NICE TO HAVE:

SALMON
SALAD DRESSINGS
     1. ITALIAN
     2. RANCH   } CAN BE INEXPENSIVE
     3. CAESAR

CHILI BEANS – 3 CANS

BLACK BEANS—1 CAN	BLACK OLIVES—1 CAN
TOMATO SAUCE 6 SMALL CANS	GREEN OLIVES—1 JAR
TOMATO PASTE 2 SMALL CANS	ARTICHOKES—1 JAR

MUSROOMS – 4 SMALL CANS

JALAPENOS –SMALL CAN

VEGETABLES 3 –4 CANS GREEN BEANS, SPINACH & MIXED & CORN (One of each can do)

PANCAKE SYRUP-ANY KIND

PEPPERONI IN PACKAGE

1-2 PORK AND BEANS

CREAMED SOUPS: 3-4 Cream of Mushroom, Cream of Celery & Cream of Chicken and Plain Tomato Soup. (These, what ever is on sale)

SPICES/MUST HAVES:	NICE TO HAVE:
BAY LEAF	
SALT (Big Box)	CUMIN
PEPPER (Big Box)	TACO SEASONING PACKETS (sale)
GARLIC POWDER (Large)	BASIL
OREGANO OR	
MIXED ITALIAN SPICES TARRAGON	
CHILI POWDER	ROSEMARY
CINNAMON	ALL OTHERS
DRY COCOA POWDER	All above usually from my garden!
SAGE	

DAIRY

MARGARINE QUARTERS – 1 LB.	CHEESE – 8 OZ. SOLID BLOCK
BUTTER – 1 LB.	1 – 2 (MOZARELLA)
MILK OR DRY MILK PACKETS (Usually makes 2 quarts)	

To start, I do a grocery shopping that includes a list of all of the above items or only some to restock what I have used from these items in the month that has passed. I have figured out that the first time I bought all of the items on the list, my bill was $89 in a generic food store. (I call a generic food store, a store where you bag your own groceries, not a membership store where you buy in quantity). If we got out a lot and I have a lot of staples still on the shelf, I only spend $35—$45 dollars from month to month to replace what I have used. It is then that I can spend more money on fresh food items like meat, vegetables and fruit.

But I often replace quickly used items like tomato sauce, paste, tomatoes and canned mushrooms. Sugar, rice, and canned beans, kidney and black are almost always on this list. In the winter creamed canned soups or tomato soups go a little faster and can be bought for well less than one third of the price in a generic store than our most popular Super Markets. There are items I use for cooking like canned spinach, peas, veg-all types of mixes and certain canned fruits for baking or glazes (like canned apricots) that I add to my shelf at a time when my grocery staple bill is low. Also evaporated milk and dry milk packets that can be used in a pinch or in baking. Milk made of Dry Milk can be made into buttermilk with the use of a little lemon juice. These items are invaluable when it comes to making a quick coffee bread out of a store's own brand of "Bisquick" mix that is ready to go without adding baking powder or raising yeast dough. Conveniences like this come up with favorites like "Velvet Crumb Cake" or just plain coffeecake by using the oven for warmth and pleasant odors for appetites while roasting other oven foods.

Spices are added to the larder when on sale once or twice a year at Family Dollar or Walgreen's or seasonally from the Garden, after drying them and using empty small containers I've saved from other things to store and label them. Things like extracts for baking and baking powder or soda are usually never on sale, so I buy them only at the most trendy generic type stores where you do your own bagging, etc. In these stores, I can buy simple extracts but the choices and varieties are highly limited. Popular supermarkets never have extracts on sale, if only rarely, around the holidays.

There is also room on my list for some notes to add when I check the weekly sale flyers if the item can be gotten cheaper that week at another store. These things I watch like a hawk so I can keep my family happy with the level of creating enjoyable meals and snacks on a regular basis.

But these same ethnic stores are the place to stock up on meat and poultry to keep a well diversified freezer at the lowest possible price. A freezer with an inexpensively stocked variety of meat items can add to the joy of cooking exciting meals often at the touch of opening a freezer door to find sale pot roast cut up by myself and ready for Hungarian Goulash, or sale Chicken Breasts for Mole.

So, staples are put on a running list over my kitchen counter and I purchase them all year long on a monthly basis. This, is the basis for savings. But, the real savings comes in with the weekly sale papers for fresh vegetable, fruit and meats. These are what I stock my freezer with in the way of Meat and Chicken in order to make the most nutritious meals with the least amount of expense.

Whenever I collect cheap pork chop slices for my freezer, and cheap generic store "sale" boxed stuffing mix, I can glue together a Pork Roast anytime by making up the stuffing on top of the stove and then putting a tablespoon of stuffing over each chop with a slice of apple in between. After the chops are assembled, I stand them straight up like a roast, cover it with coarse ground salt, black coarse ground pepper, caraway seed, and a little garlic powder. If I have any apple left over I decorate the top of the slices (now a standing pork roast made up of end cut pork chops). Because of the fat of the pork chops, and the seasonings, dressing and apple, this Roast is sometimes more scrumptious than an expensive Pork Roast and often preferred by my family to one. And, you can make it anytime you have the ingredients stocked away. Also, because of the fatty slices, a crispier finished product is presented.

If I buy a pound of shrimp on sale, I put a few (4 or so) away to trim a future seafood dish or float atop a seafood bisque. The same for a bulk of fish, whether it must be bought that way for a sale price or I have bought more than what we can eat at one meal. We don't really go crazy over eating leftover fish. Also, I can use these two pieces in a nice mixed grill, along with a piece of salmon, my four saved shrimp and a few fresh scallops to make a "look-forward-to" Lenten meal, not a duty diet or typical Friday meal!

The look of what you cook, the color, the combinations of what is put together, like my cheapest Pork Roast, makes the meal worth cooking and eating. With the dressing, apples, spices and crispness, it is the apple of a diner's eye when they sit down hungry. With a gravy boat of Cream of Mushroom Soup that has been poured over the roast at the beginning and rendered as gravy from the bottom of the roast at the end, it cannot be beat for flavor with the natural gravy. Add a meal sized order of instant mashed potatoes for 4 – 6 people and you have a feast with leftovers galore that can be microwave the next day. I always buy cucumbers when they are on sale and make cucumbers with sour cream (yogurt) with this dish. It is so easy and always good and compliments well. It can also be served the next day without doing anything but perhaps stirring it once.

I have mentioned that I can buy pasta at certain stores for as little as 4/$1.00. I try to buy the most uncommon looking types that they have, because I find that different textures of foods excite peoples palates when presented with a familiar dish. If you buy short stubby macaroni in one package, baby egg drops (pastina) in another, spirele in still another and rotini; you can cook two different varieties since the packages are small and serve both as choices under a Pepper Steak, Goulash or Paprikash dish. It makes for more interesting food and dinner conversation as well as guests or family feeling special when they dig in, like the shapes of starch to hide under their gravy!

Using a whole chicken can be much more interesting if you clip off the back bone and wings to make some chicken soup for an appetizer from the same chicken you will serve stuffed with wild rice or ethnic stuffing. If you are doing two chickens it is much easier to do a soup out of a few pieces; But if you are only doing one and you feel the pieces have not given the broth enough chicken flavor, Chicken Bouillon cubes are good to complete the soup with a little parsley. Whatever, of course, you have in the way of vegetables on hand, if not fresh, canned Veg-All, etc. (probably put in the beginning of this production, with the chicken pieces). There is always a way to make what you have stretch and therefore, make it a more impressive meal, even if it be just for family.

In the chapters ahead, I will share recipes and more illuminating culinary secrets of 40 years of inventing eatery very inexpensively, yet yummy and luscious, often with only the change in a jar.

If you have found yourself lately with more time on your hands than money, you will love my little cookbook! Shopping is key and taking the awareness in markets that markets consistently make high color nutrients available at low dollar prices. This alone can start a whole new life trend enjoying your leisure time creating things you love to eat, learning some gourmet secrets, while saving yourself some cash, and even pounds.

CHAPTER THREE

THE GARDEN

I don't know to what extent you actually depend on your garden for the 'piece de resistance' of fresh vegetables from June to November. I try to get the biggest bang for my season on what is the easiest and most prolific to grow.

Spinach and lettuce arrive early and can be replanted when they dwindle and brown in the heat of July so they are valuable all season. On the other hand, greens like Kale and Leek grow all summer long and can be used from June to almost November in some cases. Tomatoes, of course, we must wait a little longer for, but when started in a pot inside their yield can be tasted as early in June. Cabbages and green beans can yield over and over all summer if the cabbage is dusted with baby powder to keep away bugs and the beans are picked everyday to keep the flowers coming. Several crops must be planted about a week apart during the planting season. Cucumbers have the highest yield, it seems, in my garden. They can be picked all summer for instant salad if started early in the house and then put in an ideal climbing space with a fence or trellis where they can grow undisturbed. But alas, they are the only vegetable which I have figured out no way to freeze . . . . only pickle. (Even with the instructions of a sophisticated gardening book that I used for years that came under the heading of the First Organic Garden, I couldn't really freeze them and get them to be crisp in a salad, more like pickled pickles).

Herbs are amazing spectacle to watch grow and I have a special section next to my gazebo where I grow all of my spices for the whole year. I can see them from where I sit reading my Sunday paper. Many spices are perennials and come back with very little work or prompting. Sage, chives, some tarragon's and basil, although not all perennial (except for sage) have often made a come back because of the location not being altered for years. This may be due to seeds staying in the same area.

There was a time when I always arrived as a guest at Christmas holidays with home baked bread or cookies or wine, but now I tote a spice plant hosts can watch all the bleak winter in their sunniest window. Also, they can then enjoy the fruits of using the spice all summer. If a plant cannot be used I bring the rewards of my own spice Garden in a jar. It is surprising what a house hostess gift like this can inspire.

Once, when presented with one of my finest jars of already picked and dried basil, my husband's cousin, who was hosting the Christmas party, went into her spice cabinet and brought out tons of spices she hadn't used for years. She sent me home with a heaping bag of Cream of Tartar, Ginger, Cumin, Caraway seeds, Celery seed and a bag of herbal tea to boot. She said while she adored Garden grown basil, the other containers were taking up space and probably getting old. She didn't really know anyone else that was interested in cooking enough to get rid of them on; so I went home with a treasure trove!

Once upon a time, in my late twenties, when we first bought our house, I had a Polish neighbor who had a canning pot in her basement. Together, in summer, we canned once a week, on Tuesday, my day off from the restaurant where I worked. It was great for me because I was a little leery of opening the hot water bath after the cooking process after hearing that once in a while they exploded. But here was my neighbor, Jenny, in command just as though she were back in Poland, still doing her Mother's Canning process, with the experience of 40 years of opening the hot water bath and twisting the jars tight for the winter of sauces, soups, and chili to come.

Mostly, it was with great pride and joy that I used the tomatoes all winter in my spaghetti sauces and soups; not to mention the money I saved myself to spend on things like ingredients for Baked Alaska and Walnuts for the family Strudel we call Potitsa.

Now, I am afraid to can without her and instead cook my tomatoes down and freeze the sauce in small marked containers in one corner of my freezer. For whole tomatoes I stack them up whole in another corner of the freezer for sauces and soups all through the winter. Sometimes, if I really like a variety of tomato, I use the frozen seeds again, if the yield is really good.

Once, I saved seeds from a variety of really huge cherry tomatoes, and they took over my Gazebo so much so that they grew over the roof and used the picket wooden walls as their own tomato cage. That year I made so much sauce and other tomato dishes like Tomato bisque and Soup, that I never had to buy even one tomato product all winter. And because they took such hold of my gazebo, which was twenty degrees hotter than outside of it, they grew until December 3rd or so. It was truly a Gardener's phenomenon, and we felt as though we were showered upon with Roman tomato manna from the heavens. That year there were tomatoes on my kitchen table until March.

Squashes can be almost as surprising although they take forever to mature. I let them roll along the back of my garden, their heavy leaves supporting the larger varieties of tomato plants I used to can. When they finally bloom, I use the flowers to deep fry. They are like a delicious Italian delicacy. A delicacy I learned from my Italian neighbor who claimed they fed her country under Mussolini's years of dictatorship. If these exotic delicacies sustained a generation of otherwise starving Sicilian's the more respect to this plant, I say. Of course, the final result is always a surprise in my Garden from the years of squash planting in the back of the yard.

Sometimes old squash seeds get mixed in with new ones and I have tripped over an overgrown watermelon or cantaloupe while harvesting zucchinis for my fall Zucchini bread. Sometimes, in years past, I have even baked a young watermelon thinking it was a different kind of squash. To my family's surprise, it was delicious and sweet without anything but butter. When one day I tripped over a hidden fully grown watermelon in the same area, I knew then that I had been baking young watermelon all summer. I wondered sometimes, if these kinds of accidents had also sustained the Sicilians before they deep-fried their first squash blossoms.

Young zucchini are summer meal accompaniments, but the older and larger ones that hide at the bottom of my back squash garden are great for Zucchini bread and sometimes yield 4 to 8 loaves a squash. It is a joy to find them hiding in late August. Even with a squirrel bite or two on them, they are a joy to trip over as I look to see the progress of my young pumpkins.

Fruit trees, of course, if you have them, are the most valuable of any yield in a home garden. My neighbors apple and pear trees hung over my fence for years. It was with much delight when she told me to keep my own side of the fence clean, that I picked up ripe fruit from the ground in my yard all season everyday, and sometimes less ripe fruits from the branches when I was determined to bake a pie or make a Jell-O mold recipe for Easter that calls for lime Jell-O, cream cheese, pecans and fresh pears. AS for the fruits on the ground, they never went to waste in my house for jams and preserves. But when my neighbors moved the new neighbors who purchased the home next door cut the trees down and put up high fences, blocking out their yard from our view. It was the first time in twenty years that I had to buy an apple or a pear in a store, and it was very strange. I begrudged buying them!

I still receive figs from yet another neighbor, who buries her fig tree under the ground all winter by bending it and covering it with compost and dirt. These are the figs I have become used to ripening on my windowsills and using for baking for thirty years. When I see fresh figs in the store and the prices they ask for them, I am amazed and grateful and hope my neighbor will be around a little longer for her generosity. Fresh resources like apples, pears, and figs are an invaluable commodity in food value and for their fresh tastes in food preparations. Although there can never be enough of goods like this, I see that I have never even had an inkling of buying a fruit tree for my own yard and I don't really know why. Maybe the work. They require a lot of pruning and spraying. Last year we put in blueberry and raspberry bushes, so we will see what happens this summer, as they take two years to yield.

If ever I would begin a fruit tree, I have always thought it would be cherry. My Mother had a cherry tree in a very urban neighborhood for years for which she did absolutely no upkeep. First of all, the flowers are beautiful. And, when they were really in bloom we picked them from the second floor porch adjacent to her two flat apartment. Her Grandchildren still remember the fun we had, not to mention the constant cherry jams, tarts, pies and fresh snacks they enjoyed all summer just a few feet away.

Strawberries have always been my standby stable fruit. They sometimes come back on their own and there is nothing like picking a few fresh berries every morning in the summer for your breakfast. Cantaloupes are also an easy summer time fruit to grow and they are very sweet when they are organic and not mass—produced. They grow smaller in a home garden and therefore sweeter. When I visit my daughter in the Tampa area of Florida, I am always saddened at the grapefruits, lemons and oranges on the grass that people take for granted and let go rotten on the ground. Sometimes I find myself coming home with a bag or two that last me for a month.

Whatever you decide to grow in the available space you may have, will always be a joy to you no matter how you grow it. Just seeing something grow is a daily thrill for me and being able to use it in a recipe is always another boon. I met a man in the Museum where I work who told me how to grow bean sprouts in a jar in the winter. He said that he grew them all winter long and never had to buy fresh greens for a vegetable. He made a salad from them everyday or so and was not a slave to the markets in his sophisticated North side neighborhood. I also know a woman who grows vegetables in pots all summer on the porch steps of her apartment in a sophisticated Lake Shore neighborhood.

Being a woman, I enjoy the markets and produce in the ethnic stores where I live. Some are close to the swimming pool at a YMCA that is near my home where I swim my mile everyday. I enjoy stopping to see their "in store" specials like 50 cent pints of strawberries or 99 cent blueberry sales, as well as many "in store" meat items like 29 or 39 cent chicken leg quarters. Sometimes, if I am really lucky I can find a package of Pollack for $1.00 that is marked down for quick sale. These, so reasonable, make me feel that I cannot afford NOT to go into the store at least every other day. It also makes me feel like I live in a little Village in a country where people market daily for their supper. A place where existing almost only on Change in a jar is fun.

CHAPTER FOUR

THE WONDERS OF REFRIGERATED BISCUITS

The first encounter with this wonder cost me all of eight cents. It was the day after walking the streets of a small town looking for Chicago style pizza in a town that didn't have a pizza of any kind. Except, that is at a Tastee Freeze where they offered slices of a pie shaped bread with loose hamburger on it and no cheese, and a non-Italian style tomato sauce.

Well, for Chicago folks, this just will not do. Not for four more years of being in a town like Peru, Indiana. Ballard refrigerated biscuit dough used to be 10 cents in 1964. But sometimes, it was on sale for 8 cents. It was then I would buy 4 or 5 of them and save them in the refrigerator for our Friday night pizza party in our huge kitchen on 6th Street.

I would roll out the ten biscuits as thin as I could, maybe about 12 inches each, like the individual pizzas that restaurants sell now days. Then I would take an 8 oz. Can of plain old tomato sauce and doctor it up with oregano, pepper, garlic powder and whatever else I had in the spice rack my Mother-in-law gave me as a Christmas present. One can, believe it or not actually, spread thin, cover 10 little pizza dough biscuit rollings with the help of a little addition of ketchup to stretch the amount of Italian sauce. After the tomato sauce, I loaded my individual pies with a half pound of crumbled hamburger from the 49 cents a pound hamburger I bought at Bailey's Butcher Market, in a once a month bulk of 10 pounds when we got our Airforce payroll check.

I would mix anise seed, oregano, basil and garlic into the ½ pound of meat and sprinkle it over my little pies. Then I would take onion, green pepper and tomato, or whatever else I had in my little diaper dryer vegetable garden where I only had enough space to dry my baby diapers out every morning and use the ground under the clothesline to grow vegetables. After the little pies were loaded with whatever was available, I shredded some fake mozzarella "cheese" they sold in the commissary out at the base in huge packages for $2.00 for 2 pounds. Once the little fellows were assembled I gave them one more sprinkle of garlic powder and thrust them into the old iron oven in my wonderful yellow kitchen that had a counter straight down the middle of it to divide the cooking part from the eating part.

In about 10 minutes or so the huge, old attic apartment smelled like Chicago pizza, delicious and mouthwatering, and 10 individual pies at a total cost of about $1.00 for all of them together. My husband and I would each eat about three and split a quart of Carling's Black Label Beer. The baby was still on formula and baby food so we saved the four precious remaining pizzas for a snack for the next day. And, I always made them on a Friday night, because on Saturday afternoon, after lunch, they were gone. My new meal, which was usually Pork Steak, a Saturday night special which cost me about 50 cents in total for a pound was a special Saturday night treat. I would broil them and make a few baked potatoes, so it was special. And another can of biscuits got baked. This time as dinner rolls.

My amazement at becoming a cook out of quick necessity after our marriage move of location to a small town in Indiana, amazed me even more with each revelation of overwhelming success in learning to cook delicious meals from a cookbook with little expense. Of course, I had some real disappointments from remembering how I bought groceries for my Mother for say, 50 cents for a pound of liver or hamburger or halibut at the end of the week when our food supply sort of dwindled. Once, in my new life, I bought some pork kidneys for kidney stew for only 29 cents for a whole pound. I followed a recipe and even though it seemed OK over a bed of rice with the sauce and all, I noticed I never bought kidneys again or tried to repeat the dish with beef kidneys or another recipe. A real disaster was mistakenly buying Pork liver instead of Beef liver. The smell alone after it was cooked, kept us from being able to eat it at all and we ended up eating a can of Pork and Beans for supper at the end of the month, waiting for our check. Delicious after Pork kidney stew!

But, for the most part, my cooking experiments were pretty successful. I once got the idea to bake bread once a month and fill the freezer with enough bread to last the whole month. It was well worth the effort and saved us the trip to the store where we always spent more than we planned on a run just for bread.

Also, I began to become innovative about cooking and planning meals. Once, when we had no dessert for a long, long, time I fried the Refrigerated biscuits and shook them in a bag of sugar, and we had hot donuts. They tasted like the Punchke we grew up on and later, I found out from my Mother, that the dough was really just the same as what she used to make Punchke on Fat Tuesday, the day before Ash Wednesday in Lent.

After that, I would make them often for company and when a woman would frequently ask for the recipe, I would preface it by saying "You're going to just love this recipe". And of course, when they would find out all it was, they did. Sometimes I would vary the recipe by trying to inject jelly into them to make "Jelly Biscuits" out of them, or pull them into long rectangles to make "Long John's" frosted with icing (made out of plain powder sugar" and milk) just like in the bakery.

As successful this dessert was for our tastes and to throw at company, just when they thought the party was over, there was ever still another use for these little biscuits . . . . Giant Popovers! Yes, I would pinch two or three of them together and Walla . . . . a Popover as big as your fist came out of the oven to serve with Beef Stew or Scrambled eggs for a Brunch. It never failed to amaze me what could be done with these wonderful little biscuits. I still use them to this day in all the ways I have just mentioned. Also, I have used them as a topping to cover a Chicken and Dumpling dish I make with an oven stewed Chicken at the end of the recipe. It makes the dish complete and your guests amazed at what trouble you took to engage their appetite's visual expectations of whatever you put on the table.

Once, I saw some brie on sale at a generic grocery store (where you have to bag your own items) for 2 for $1.00 and bought all I could gather up. About 20 of them in all! Everytime I had company, all I had to do was grab a package of brie out of the fridge, wrap it with a few biscuit rolls, bake it and trim it with some veggies on the side and crackers; or whatever I could find to make the appetizer platter look appealing with the hot brie in the middle. Sometimes just a few carrot and celery sticks and crackers would suffice alongside something that looked so special in the middle of the platter. If I was serving something Mexican, I would pour salsa over the top of the cooked covered cheese and place homemade (3 for $1.00 avocado) guacamole on a huge mound across from it on the platter and trim with a surround of some Dollar Store Corn Chips. What at feast! And happy guests who think you have slaved all day for their company!

Although refrigerated biscuits do not cost 10 cents anymore, they can be gotten for about $1.00 for a package of 5 at a generic food store. They still taste as good (especially the buttermilk ones) as ever if used in combination with these arrangements or sometimes just pinched together for thickness and baked in the oven as an accompaniment as hot rolls to a dinner. They still are cheaper than buying prepared dinner roll packages or slaving all day over biscuit dough. Just see what you can wrap them around, like a plain old hot dog and bake them in the oven after putting a little mustard and honey on them before the actual wrapping and baking!

They make something so plain look like you really cared!

CHAPTER FIVE

APPETIZERS

In a day and age when appetizers have become mini meals in a restaurant and/or meals in themselves that can be bought in freezer cases, sophisticated and laden with calories like fried cheese sticks and mini-tacos and cheese coated pretzels and mini-pizzas, it is hard to satisfy company with what appetizers really were set out once to be . . . . .just something to whet the appetite. Not a calorie laden start to a calorie laden main meal.

They can be attractive and appetizing without the fullness of a meal and still go well with cocktails. Serving potato chips with dips as an appetizer is not innovative or an appetite enhancement. This kind of fare is a cheap snack food in my books and tastes and really shows a lack of interest to introducing the main meal.

Using raw vegetables has been an answer in later years to all the chip and dip calories and combinations of appetizers. Even tortilla chips and salsa are a healthier answer when it comes to the beginning of a Mexican meal. But they are not really anything special for company when they can be bought in a store minutes before company arrives.

There are so many wonderful and pleasing appetizers that can enhance a cocktail period before the main dinner. Caring and creative can be truly delicious for as little as less than paying for a high salt chips and fatty dips. Some will go as far as buying humus dips to put out on veggie platters with the cocktail hour. This, I can appreciate for being a health food nut! But, really there are so many ambrosial and appealing snacks that don't take as much time, as a run to a store with a list.

For instance, stuffed celery. There is a dip that I mix out of osterized creamy cottage cheese and then add chopped olives to one part, chopped pineapple to another and shrimp sauce to another. I lather it on crisp celery lengths that have been in water during the night. The crispness makes filling easy to apply to the celery. The choices are colorful, low in calories, healthy and non-fattening. If you don't have a jar of olives, chopped tomatoes can be used or red or green onion.

These lengths of celery can be surrounded by a festive platter of crunchy carrot curls and radish flowers that have also been in a water bath in the fridge overnight. (Getting curly and flowery after scraping carrot curls quickly (and thickly) with a potato peeler and cutting petals into radishes before soaking). They add color and healthy decoration to the filled celery sticks. To save time, cut celery into three times larger than bite size lengths so they can be filled after soaking upright overnight in an empty cottage cheese or yogurt container. They can be cut after filling.

Creamy cottage cheese has a wonderful taste mixed with a few ingredients, once osterized into a dip. In a pinch you can use onion soup packets if you don't have time to chop any vegetables, olives or fruit.

Also, stuffed fresh mushrooms (hopefully on sale) can be made only with the stems of the mushrooms (not with ground beef or sausage as in most recipes of this kind) that are chopped and sautéed with onion and any vegetables you may have in the house. Also just Italian Seasoning or Rosemary is good mixed in with the sautéed stems. Once put this mixture back into the hole in the mushroom, just quickly grease the bottom of each mushroom with your hand with garlic powdered low fat margarine or butter while laying them out on the tray. Bake them at 400 degrees for 10 or 15 minutes or until you can smell them. Then turn them out onto an appetizer platter. This is an excellent hot appetizer and can be trimmed with a few bacon strips.

Also, broiled pineapple with brown sugar sprinkled over it can be used to trim this hot appetizer. For that matter, any fruit that is firm enough to be broiled with a little brown sugar over it can be used. Once this fruit broils enough to stand up with a little crispiness around your mushrooms, it makes an attractive and healthy platter served with a side dish of the health like dip; made of osterized cottage cheese, plain Greek yogurt humus; or salsa. Whatever brightens up the color of this hot appetizer!

Nuts are a good and healthful appetizer or can be mixed with the recipe that is given on a box of Chex cereal and baked in the oven to serve alongside a hot appetizer like stuffed mushrooms. (This recipe is almost always on the box around the holidays or the Cereal Company can be contacted for instructions.) The taste and appearance are well worth the mixing for a well-presented and healthy side dish!

If you really want to impress your guests on a low budget, just pop a 16 oz. Can of Pink Salmon into a bowl with a large package of lite cream cheese and whip it with a mix master until smooth and consistent in Salmon color. Surround with cucumber slices and other colorful carrot sticks, yellow and green zucchini rounds and plunk a shrimp dip into the center of the platter. My Shrimp dip is nothing more than a little Greek plain yogurt mixed with a little prepared shrimp sauce or catsup mixed with a little horseradish to taste.

RECIPE—SALMON DIP OR MOLD

Canned salmon which amounts to a whopping cost of $2.00 for a large can, can be made into a wonderful Salmon dip with one package of low fat cream cheese whipped with a mix-master until the mixture is of a consistent salmon color. Any kind of crackers or vegetables can be placed around the dip. The dip can be shaped and elongated like the whole salmon you often see on brunch tables in restaurants with lemon slices or wedges around it, and cream cheese slices. And maybe some cocktail sauce somewhere on the platter. If salmon is put into a ring mold, in the center hole. As above.

RECIPE – PERFECT, ZESTY, APPETIZER MEATBALLS

Tiny meatballs can be made from just one pound of frozen turkey from a generic store. Add a can of onion soup and a cup of Italian bread crumbs; a little anise, shaped into miniature meatballs and throw into the oven for 25 to 30 minutes at 375 degrees. A dip for these can be made out of BBQ sauce and Grape Jam mixed together. It's a great taste variation. Don't forget to put out some toothpicks either in each Meatball or somewhere close so folks know to dip!

I have invented a wonderful appetizer made out of a can of artichokes that costs about $2.00 these days, goes a long way, and will surprise any guest with it's deliciousness and diversity.

ARTICHOKE PUFFS

8 SLICES RYE BREAD

SPREAD SLICES WITH GARLIC BUTTER OR MARGARINE SPREAD

MIX: LG. PKG. LITE CREAM CHEESE

4 TABLS. ROMANO/PARMESAN CHEESE
1 JAR QUARTERED ARTICHOKE HEARTS
1 CAN BLACK OLIVES SLICED
½ TO 1 TUBE ANCHOVY PASTE

OPTIONAL: CAPERS

   GREEN OLIVES CHOPPED THIN

SPREAD OVER BREAD SLICES
QUARTER SLICES
BROIL UNTIL BROWN ON TOPS

(I USE OLD PIE PANS TO LAYER THEM ON AND BROIL SO THEY CAN BE EASILY REMOVED FROM BROILER PAN.)

I PLACE THEM OUT ON COLORFULLY LINED PLATTERS (NAPKINS OR PAPER DOILIES CAN LINE PLATTERS FOR THIS HOT APPETIZER)

This next adventure in Appetizers is so yummy and varied, it will do you for the rest of your life when in a pinch or just plain entertaining with a flourish!

My best girlfriend who is like a Sister to me came from Czechoslovakia. Her Mother made these for every party she had in her home, assembling them factory style from her little Czech kitchen that was on the second floor of their apartment.

Then, she used them sometimes as entree food, but when they moved to a larger house in the suburbs, I noticed they had then taken their new role as appetizers. Then, the main meal was catered Czech Food.

They are an absolute delight to make – creative and colorful and good, pleasing all tastes so much so that one can watch party goers going back to the platters of Bavarians over and over until they have tasted every combination of flavors and ingredients. Kids love making them. My husband and I have enjoyed making them for events and even wakes. They seem like a lot of work the first time you assemble them, but once you have a pattern and know what good you have in your fridge that will compliment the Bavarians, it becomes a matter of organization and a willing helper who kind of enjoys being creative.

BASIC BAVARIAN SETUP:

2 THIN, VERY FRESH, FRENCH OR ITALIAN BREAD LOAVES SLICED IN DIAGNOLS. (SHOULD GET ABOUT 20 – 30 SLICES OUT OF EACH LOAF OR MORE)

SPREAD: CAN BE PLAIN MARGARINE OR BUTTER, CREAM CHEESE OR YE OLD TAVERN CHEDDAR OR VELVEETA.

MARGARINE MIXED WITH CHIVES

CREAM CHEESE MIXED WITH CHOPPPED GREEN OLIVES

YE OLD TAVERN CHEESE SPREAD OR LIKE CHEESE SPREAD FROM A GENERIC STORE TOPPED WITH CRUSHED PRETZELS OR ½ TO 1 LB. HAM

SLICED AND QUARTERED AMERICAN, CHEDDAR, SWISS OR ANY TYPE CHEESE

6 BOILED EGGS, SLICED

SALAMI, SUMMER SAUSAGE, BEER SAUSAGE OR ANY OF THIS TYPE OF LUNCH MEAT TYPE SAUSAGE THAT CAN BE SLICED REGULAR OR THIN.

SLICED DILL PICKLE

OPTIONAL SLICED INGREDIENTS:

    PIECES OF TOMATO (LIKE 8THS CUT INTO 4 PCs)
    SLICED GREEN OLIVES OR SLICED SARDINE PIECES
    PICKLED MUSHROOM
    PICKLED HERRING (NOT CREAMED)

Nancy Dybek Greene

INSTRUCTIONS:

I start with the spread on each piece, then the piece of meat, the cheese at an opposite angle to the meat (you want the ingredients to fan out over the piece of bread and look nice and twice as large as the piece of bread).

Next, the half or quarter of egg slice (I slice these with the metal egg slicer that makes them uniform, hold them in my hand after I quarter them until I get each piece put onto a piece of bread slide, since once put down they will fall apart).

Next, the pickle slice, then the olive slice until every piece has the same ingreidients arranged in a different way or, you can make them all different by using only certain ingredients over the cheese spread, like olive, mushroom, tomato and herring. Certain ingredients over the margarine spread, like ham, cheese, pickle & egg. Other certain ingredients over the cream cheese with olive spread like salami, pickle, egg, olive & pimento.

In this way you create a certain taste with each combinationo that is consistent only with that spread. Party goers will enjoy tasting the consistency and variety of each different flavor combination, or creat your own spreads combinations and ingredients based on this basic recipe. Really, anything you may have in you refriegerator can go on them.

Once, in a pinch, I used slices of hot dogs and put a honey mustard dijon over the basic margarine spread! The kids, well everyone went wild over them, expecially with the sweet pickle slice! Get creative with whatever your refrigerator dictates! There have been times when i did not make them for a party and people asked me "where are the bavarians?" They were looking forward to a new creation.

If you really want to impress your company with something TRENDY and ususally expensive, all of the above are wonderful and can be mixed and matched with cold or hot, whatever you feel like presenting. If you want an impressive variety of color to go alongside any of these, the following can be thrown together on a lazy Susan type platter and usually costs about at least $25.00 to order in a supermarket catering Department.

ITALIAN ANTIPASTO

½ PACKAGE GENERIC STORE PEPPERONI
½ JAR PEPERONCINI – RED AND GREEN MILD PEPPERS
½ POUND MOZARELLA OR PROVOLONE CHEESE CUT INTO DIAGNOLS
ARTICHOKE HEARTS QUARTERED (FROM MARINATED JAR)
¼ LB OF ANY HAM, ITALIAN OR AMERICAN

BROCCOLI OR ASPARAGUS OR MINI-PICKLED CORNS,
GRAPE TOMATOES OR ALL

DIPPING SAUCE IN MIDDLE:
 1 TUBE ANCHOVY PASTE MIXED WITH 8 0Z SOUR CREAM

DELICIOSO!

This next creation is a tried and true recipe I have served for years to satisfied Martini and Wine drinkers.

It is reasonable to make, a good source of iron, and rich enough to go a long way before dinner. A few shaved red or regular onions atop and a garlic or onion round underneath and your on your way to soak up your Extra dry Martini or Wine.

Nancy Dybek Greene

2ND CITY CHOPPED CHICKEN LIVERS

A POUND OF CHICKEN LIVERS sautéed with chopped onion and mashed. Finely chopped onion (Enough to mash into livers for taste)

2 HARD BOILED EGGS
2 TBS. MAYONNAISE
1 TSP. WORCESTERSHIRE & Juice of 1 lemon
CHOPPED CHICKEN LIVERS
SAUTE CHICKEN LIVERS
ADD ALL OTHER INGREDIENTS AND CHILL AT LEAST 2 HOURS

SERVE WITH GARLIC AND ONION ROUNDS & FINE SHAVED ONION ATOP.

BON APPETIZER!

SCAMPI CROSTINI

2 CLOVES GARLIC ANCHOVY PASTE
CRUSHED RED PEPPER 1 LB. SHRIMP
PINOT GRIGIO PARSLEY & CHOPPED ONION

POUR OVER: Oven Toasted Garlic Bread Rounds (small size loaf)

SCRUMPTIOUS

CHAPTER SIX

PORRIDGES AND POTAGES

Hot comfort combinations of foods cooked together for their flavors and satisfying thickness on a cold winter's day gives a body that stick-to-the-ribs feeling for the energy that winter takes to "Bear down" as we people in Chicago have been known to say. Just smelling the aroma all day to anticipate indulging in dinner affords hours of looking forward. The end enjoyment of a scrumptious potage may be mouthwatering from aromas and expectation. Or maybe a taste long denied over a summer of salad eating, sandwiches and grilled foods. I have my favorites and they can make winter delightful while shoveling snow arduously myself or treating the kids after their snow day.

My Mother made Chicken Soup every Sunday along with Roast Chicken that, in those days sometimes had unlaid Chicken eggs still in it. Always, the soup had Chicken livers, and gizzards and vegetables and whatever kluski (egg noodle) my Mother bought or made by hand. For Sunday after church dinner, we feasted on the scrumptious Roasted Chicken. But on Sunday evening, we had the soup with sandwiches made from Polish cold cuts my Father bought fresh every Sunday. Tongue, and Roast Pork loin and whatever we put in our order for, before he made his trip to the Polish Deli. On Sunday's I still get a terrible taste for Chicken Soup at any time of year! My Mother often had Ham lunch meat leftover from the Neisner's 5 & 10 she sent me to on Saturday, where they sold their Ham for 50 cents @ lb. She always got one dollar's worth, so two pounds, along with a loaf of rye bread that was 35 cents. This was our Saturday lunch treat. Leftover ham was for our weekday school lunch boxes.

On Saturday night, my Mother always made a family size sirloin steak, baked potatoes and peas. She would cut the steak in strips when she served it, like she saw the chef do in the country club where she worked as a hostess. The baked potatoes were flouted in a fancy way my Mother had also seen at the Country Club. So, we not only ate well in our house, but food was served with great care and creativity. Even though I was very young, I noticed that my girlfriends Mother's never served any food with the graciousness of my own Mother' serving. And, they even did things like put plastic bowls filled with mashed potatoes on the table, which was a great NO NO from my Mother's kitchen. No plastic plates or bowls allowed and often (providing it was something that could be dry enough to serve this way, like pastry) she put a paper doilie under the food.

My Mother's serving ethics have never left me or my dining-room-table. And me, with my three sets of China! And . . . . multiple and various silver or crystal like or "stunning—on-the-table" serving dishes collected trying to see the world. Or gifts my Aunt Elsie has given me as special serving pieces she has found in the finest of China departments, from her shopping trips to Marshall Fields and Mikasa's warehouse..

My Mother's thoughtfulness to make simple food, not only appetizing, but elegant. There is a quality in presentation that makes people feel special. Most of the following recipes were in her repertoire or her own Mother's while others evolved during my lifetime as chief cook and bottle washer in our own household.

POTAGES

I am going to start with the potages that are more like soups than meals and are quite inexpensive and simple. All, however, can be served as either.

POTATO BISQUE WITH LEEK

3 quarts of Water in Large Soup Pot
10 potatoes of any kind, preferably red
1 large bunch of leek (a bunch green onions can be substituted)
1 – 2 cups instant mashed potatoes (if you prefer thick soups as I do)
4 Chicken Bouillon Cubes
1 tsp. Salt
1 tsp. Black pepper

Cook all ingredients except Instant Mashed Potatoes and bouillon cubes for 45 minutes to 1 hour.

Add Instant mashed Potatoes after Soup has finished melding of flavors and potatoes are mostly cooked down, but do not mash. Leave in hunks. Add bouillon cubes also at this time and cook until melted into soup.

When ladling out the delicious soup, I snip fresh chives over each serving in the summer. In the winter, I sprinkle some Rosemary or Tyme or both if you like the taste together or grate a little cheddar cheese over it. Sometimes, if I don't have cheese with color in it, I put a little crumbled pre-cooked bacon over the top. Whatever you think will enhance the dish for you and your guests! Bon Appetite! And all for a whopping $2.00 a pot if the instant mashed potatoes are from a generic wholesale store!

I like to serve this soup with a little home made Garlic Bread. Since potato soup is not spicy, garlic bread is a marvelous accompaniment. It really makes a meal out of this presentation using fresh store bought French or Italian Bread or crusts of any bread you may have saved in your freezer or regular Sandwich bread-on-hand.

(See Garlic Bread recipe in Bread and Quick Bread Section)

TOMATO BISQUE

You will love this recipe! Colorful, delicious and impressive, all it is, is as follows.

1 OR 2 PLUM TOMATOES CUT IN 8TH'S (OR 1 CAN OF ANY STEWED VARIETY)
4 CANS CAMPBELL'S (OR ANY BRAND) TOMATO SOUP
1 CUP WHOLE MILK OR CREAM
1 CUP OR SO OF ROTINI NOODLES
3 TBS. OF FRESH OR SPICE JAR BASIL
4 BOULLION CUBES (2 BEEF & 2 Chicken)
½ pound Feta Cheese (Crumble in Soup @ End)

Follow order of ingredients, adding cooked rotini (or other small pasta, like small size shells, etc).

Add spices and bouillon cubes, cook 10 more minutes and serve with crumbled Feta (or type you make prefer) Feta, like this soup, is low fat and enhances it's pure mild deliciousness.

When I ladle the creamy red liquid soup out, I snip or sprinkle whatever green I may have over the top, even if it is more basil. It is good too with a little inexpensive Tortellini in it instead of the Rotini. With Tortellini, it may make it more of a meal. Low Fat, and tasty, it will make family or guests surprised at how plain old Tomato Soup can be not only a meal, but a special one.

I like to serve this recipe with a combination of fresh Italian Bread in a basket mixed with a few pieces of Garlic Bread. Some people prefer regular bread to the Garlic variety with this spicy soup.

FRENCH ONION SOUP

This is a soup I make only when I have Pot Roast Meat to cook in a favorite way in my electric frying pan. First I season and lightly flour the Pot Roast and sear the meat on both sides as brown as I can get it without changing the flavor into something burnt. This browning process will earn heaps of very brown soup and Pot Roast gravy. Then I simply cover with 6 – 8 Onions and 2 quarts water to start, and cook until tender, about 2 ½—3 hours in my electric frying pan on as low a heat as it will cook without shutting off automatically. I add water up to the top and keep adding water about 5 or 6 times or as often as it will take to in order to keep the water level to the top of the pan.

When the Pot Roast is cooking I remove most of the liquid with the onions. This will yield about 2 quarts of French Onion Soup. Salt and Pepper can be added to taste, but it really does not need much more than that for Seasoning if the Pot Roast is browned right.

With the remainder of the liquid, (or adding new liquid if I need) I make thick Pot Roast Gravy and pour it back over the meat in the Electric Frying Pan with a can or two of Mushrooms or a pound of fresh ones left whole.

This Soup is just too good to not try to make 2 meals out of one, while cooking a good pot roast. If I feel like serving the Onion Soup separately at a different meal, I simply put shredded cheese sprinkled with parmesan and romano and bake until melted.

It is a shame to cook a Pot Roast for three hours or so and not get this extra delicious meal out of it!

TURKEY CARCASS SOUP

Every holiday that I cook a turkey I am already thinking about this wonderful soup while the Turkey is yet roasting. Even more seriously, I am thinking about it whilst I am making the gravy, already saving the bits and pieces it leaves in the pan for my notorious gravy and this soup. The neck, which is usually discarded by others who deem it worthless, gets socked away long before anyone really sits down at the table to eat the first turkey dinner. Some of the gizzard and pieces of broken off meat from the wings or meat that is stuck to the bottom of my roasting bag is laid into a pot of turkey drippings from the bag. With this I include other pieces of turkey or vegetables or fallen out and hardened roasted dressing, that may not look suitable to go into my perfect gravy.

After the Carcass is boned, mostly at the end of the second time we have eaten Turkey for dinner after the holiday; I add all I have saved and begin to boil this mixture together in about 4 quarts of water. As the residual meat falls off the bones of the turkey and the bits of dressing and turkey neck meat become one in what starts to look like soup, I remove the carcass from the pot and let it cool. When cool enough to work with, I remove the rest of what meat might be still on the bone and throw it back into the soup. I then add some vegetables I may have left over from our holiday meal, like sweet potatoes, broccoli, asparagus or any celery that is left uncooked in the fridge that was too much for the dressing. I add to all this in the pot, 1 to 1 1/4 cup of rice depending on how big a soup pot I am using. (Be careful, even though rice tastes very good in this recipe, using more than two cups can turn out to be a solid pot of rice flavored with turkey broth and vegetables. This, as good as it may taste, might leave one feeling like it is too much heavy rice eating after heavy holiday Turkey and trimming meals.)

Rice comes off with a better flavor from Turkey broth (lighter) than from Chicken, and once my family got used to having this delicious and interesting after holiday meal a few times, (thus elongating the holiday with something we never have again all year) they really look forward to it.

If after cooking this for 1 and ½ hours and you feel that the Turkey broth is a little weak, (this depends on how well you brown your Turkey when roasting), you may want to add about four chicken bouillon cubes if you have a large pot going. The rice is also a good binder for the unusual blend of drippings, hunks of straggling vegetables or dressing or giblets, to bring the taste all together in a delicious and special annual holiday treat. It's a welcome money saver after a holiday and ultimately becomes a family tradition that changes every year depending on what you have put on the table for the Thanksgiving meal!

MOTHER–IN-LAW'S
MANHATTAN CLAM CHOWDER

My mother-in-law made this scrumptious clam chowder faithfully every Friday, as though she were feeding a bunch of hungry Truck Drivers at lunch time like her Mother who owned a Road House business in Wisconsin. It surprised me that she made this meal on Friday since she was never very fond of Seafood or anything very sophisticated.

GREEN PEPPER (1 CUP EACH)

CELERY   SAUTE IN BUTTER IN BOTTOM OF LARGE
          SOUP POT

ONION   MAKE ROUX ON TOP OF SAUTEED VEGETABLES
          & CONTINUE WITH OTHER INGREDIENTS

ADD 4-5 QUARTS WATER TO POT WITH SAUTEED VEGETABLES
POTATOES   CUBED 2 CUPS
1 CAN TOMATO SAUCE (8 oz.)
12 TSP. TYME
1/ 2 TSP SALT
1/2 TSP CRUSHED PEPPER

MAKE ROUX OF 1-2 CUP FLOUR AND 2 CUPS MILK

AFTER FRESH VEGETABLES ARE SAUTEED, ROUX IS MADE AND MIXED INTO VEGETABLES, ADD WATER AND ALL OTHER INGREDIENTS. COOK 30 – 40 MINUTES, STIRRING OFTEN TO COMBINE SMOOTHLY.

CLAM JUICE—3—6 ½ OZ. CANS OF CLAMS

CHOP 4 TOMATOES AND ADD WITH CLAMS & CLAM JUICE

COOK 20 MORE MINUTES UNTIL TASTES LIKE CLAM CHOWDER.

YOU CAN ADD BACON TO THE SAUTEEING VEGETABLES IF YOU LIKE, BUT I DON'T SINCE IT SEEMS TO TAKE AWAY THE SEAFOOD TASTE.

COLD EASTER BORSCHT

This is a cold soup and long before Easter arrives I have a terrible taste for it. It is made of ingredients that are not commonly called Borscht, but it has been in my family for years, yet I have never seen it in any Polish Cook Book nor for that matter, any cook book. There have been other families that make it in the Polish neighborhood we moved into when my daughter was in Grammar School, but no one could ever tell me what part of Poland it came from or from whom they received the recipe.

12 BOILED EGGS
1 – 2 LINKS FRESH POLISH SAUSAGE
BOIL TOGETHER UNTIL EGGS ARE HARDBOILED AND POLISH SAUSAGE IS COOKED.
HAM CUT IN 1 INCH HUNKS OR SLICES
2 8 oz. CONTAINERS LOW FAT SOUR CREAM (16oz)
2 QUARTS BUTTERMILK
GREEN ONION
1 TABLS. SALT
1 TSP. PEPPER
1 TSP DRY MUSTARD

COOK EGGS AND POLISH SAUSAGE IN 1 QUART WATER

REMOVE EGGS WHEN HARD & LEAVE WATER IN POT UNTIL POLISH IS COOKED THOROUGHLY. RESERVE LIQUID IN SAME POT AND TAKE POLISH OUT AND CUT ON SLANT IN SMALL PIECES

PEEL EGGS & SET ASIDE

CHOP GREEN ONION & GET HAM INTO SMALL MOUTHSIZE PCs. FOR BORSCHT.

COMBINE BUTTERMILK, SOUR CREAM,

SLICE EGGS INTO EIGHTS OR QUARTERS AND PUT INTO
SOUP

STIR INGREDIENTS WELL AND REFRIGERATE BEFORE
SERVING 60 MINS.

Serve cold.

Nancy Dybek Greene

SUMMER ZUCHINNI GARDEN SOUP/PUREE

1   CUP ONION

2   TABLS. BUTTER

6   CUPS SLICES ZUCHINNI

2   CHICKEN BOULLION CUBES PER 2 CUPS WATER

3   TSP. PARSLEY/ 2 TSP.GARDEN CHIVES/2 TSP. GARDEN
    ROSEMARY/BASIL

SAUTE 1 CUP ONION IN 2 TBLS. BUTTER. (IF YOU USE MARGARINE THIS RECIPE WILL NOT TASTE THE SAME UNLESS IT IS SOMETHING THAT CLAIMS IT TASTES JUST LIKE BUTTER!)

ADD 6 CUPS SLICED ZUCHINNI AND 2 CUPS WATER AND 2 CHICKEN BOUILLION CUBES UNTILL SQUASH IS DONE.

ADD PARSLEY AND OTHER DESIRED HERBS

BLEND IN BLENDER UNTIL SMOOTH.

MAY WHIP IN 3 TBSP. SOUR CREAM (OR YOGURT) IF CREAMINESS IS DESIRED

SERVE COLD AFTER REFRIGERATED AT LEAST ONE HOUR

NO CALORIES EXCEPT FOR THE ADDITION OF SOUR CREAM OR YOGURT & COOLING SUMMER DISH

NO COOKING SOUP

MARLENE'S LOW FAT HEARTY CHICKEN SOUP

My cousin Marlene was my only girl cousin. Maybe that's why I treasure this short and sweet recipe so much. My boy cousins all became writers (some famous) and so it is in fond memory to a beautiful lady, that I take out this card from my little recipe file box with the butterflies on it and look for a low fat, but delicious concoction on a rainy summer's day. She often made this low-fat delight for her children when they came home from school for lunch to take a few calories out for their days in High School sports.

1 LARGE CAN CHICKEN RICE SOUP
1 LARGE CAN CHICKEN NOODLE SOUP

PLACE CANS IN THE REFRIGERATOR UNTIL WELL CHILLED (SO THAT WHEN YOU OPEN THEM YOU CAN REMOVE THE FAT OFF THE TOP). REMOVE FAT FROM TOP OF EACH CAN WHILE COLD COMBINE AND COOK AS USUAL

Mm, mm, good, and less calories!

Combination of flavors makes for a taste that no one can identify as coming from a can!

MEAL POTAGES

HUNGARIAN BEEF GOULASH SOUP

1 ½ TABLS. BUTTER
1 POUND BONELESS BEEF ROUND OR CHUCK
CUT INTO 1 INCH CUBES
1 POUND ONIONS, PEELED AND SLICED THIN (5 CUPS)
1 TABLS. ALL PURPOSE FLOUR
3 TABLS. PAPRIKA
1 POUND SWEET RED PEPPERS CUT INTO CHUNKS (3 ½ CUPS)
1 CUP CANNED TOMATOES WITH THEIR JUICE, BROKEN UP
2 TSP. SALT
½ TSP. GROUND BLACK PEPPER

BROWN MEAT, COATED WITH FLOUR FROM SHAKING IN BAG WITH SEASONED FLOUR) IN DUTCH OVEN UNTIL MEAT LOOSES PINK COLOR.STIR IN ONIONS, REDUCE HEAT TO MODERATE AND COOK 30 MINS. LONGER, STIRRING EVERY 5 TO 6 MINUTES. ADD REMAINING INGREDIENTS AND BRING TO A BOIL OVER HIGH HEAT. COVER, REDUCE HEAT TO LOW AND SIMMER 2 HOURS UNTIL MEAT IS VERY TENDER. MAKES 5 CUPS SOUP.

CAN BE POURED OVER NOODLES, MASHED POTATOES OR RICE TO SERVE.

ONLY 220 CALORIES PER CUP.

CATFISH GUMBO

1 MED. ONION SLICED
¼ CUP BUTTER
2 TBLS. CORNSTARCH
1 CUP WATER
2 CANS TOMATOES (16OV)
1 CUP DICES GREEN PEPPER (2 MED)
2 CLOVES GARLIC CRUSHED
2 TSP. SALT
1 TSP. GROUND NUTMEG1/4 TSP. PEPPER
1 POUND CATFISH FILETS
2 PKG. (10 OZ) OKRA FROZEN

SAUTE CATFISH IN BUTTER AND GARLIC, CUT INTO PCs. WHEN COOL

IN SMALL BOWL STIR TOGETHER CORNSTARCH AND WATER. Add to onion with tomatoes green pepper, garlic, salt, nutmeg, pepper, and okra. Stir and cover Cook 1 hour.

SHRIMP OR ANY SHELLFISH MAY BE ADDED TO THIS!

SPANISH RICE SOUP
8 SLICES BACON
1 CUP CHOPPED ONION
1 CUP CHOPPED GREEN PEPPER
3 PICKLED JALAPENO PEPPERS CHOPPED
1 1 LB. CAN TOMATOES
1 ½ CUPS WATER
¾ UNCOOKED RICE
½ CUP CHILI SAUCE
1 TSP. SALT
½ TSP. PEPPER CRACKED
½ TSP. CRUSHED HOT PEPPERS (THOSE SERVED WITH PIZZA)
1 TSP. BROWN SUGAR
½ TSP. WORCESTERSHIRE SAUCE

COOK BACON UNTIL CRISP. REMOVE. Pour off half the fat. In remaining fat, cook onion and green pepper till tender, but not brown.

Add remaining ingredients. Cover and simmer 45 minutes. Crumble bacon on top. Trim with parsley. Makes 6 to 8 servings.

CHILI SOUP with TAMALES

4 QUARTS WATER
2 TABLS. CHILI POWDER
3 CANS CHILI BEANS IN SAUCE (LIKE BROOKS)
1 CAN BLACK BEANS
1 CAN STEWED TOMATOES (ANY VARIETY)
1 GREEN PEPPER
1 ONION LARGE
2 OR 3 ANCHO CHILES
4 OR 5 PICKLED JALAPENO PEPPERS
4 TO 5 CLOVES GARLIC
1 POUND COURSE (LARGE) GROUND MEAT (I USE TURKEY
SINCE THE MEAT FLAVOR REALLY DOES NOT COME INTO
THE CHILI FLAVOR MUCH)

SAUTE GARLIC, ONION AND MEAT.

ADD ALL OTHER INGREDIENTS & SIMMER 1 HOUR

8 TO 10 FROZEN CORN TAMALES (TOM/TOM, I USE COOKED
ACCORDING TO DIRECTIONS ON EACH WRAPPER)

I LADLE CHILI OVER A SLICED LENGTHWISE TAMALE IN
EACH BOWL.

Nancy Dybek Greene

CREAM OF LETTUCE/SPINACH SOUP

When we moved into our house, vegetable gardening was my fascination, since you could eat your rewards instead of just admiring and weeding them. But often, the vegetables could be so plentifully rewarding, that I had to use my imagination to use these delicious, organically grown greens. Tomatoes can be canned, corn can be frozen, anything in the cabbage family can be plucked from the vine until December, sometimes. But bountiful crops of leafy vegetables have to be used, pretty much, right away!

This WONDERFUL AND LO-CAL soup can be made all summer long and even frozen in small containers for tasty reminders of hot, summer, gardening days on a long winter's day!

SPINACH OR LETTUCE (TO THE EQUIVALENT OF 3 HEADS)
2 TABLS. BUTTER
1/1/2 TEAS. SALT
FRESHLY GROUND BLACK PEPPER
4 CUPS WATER
½ TO 1 CUP HEAVY CREAM
JUICE OF ½ TO 1 LEMON

WASH LETTUCE (IF SPINACH SOAK AND RINSE)

COOK FOR 10 MINUTES IN SALTED WATER

DRAIN AND CHOP

MELT BUTTER IN SAUCEPAN

ADD GREENS AND COOK 5 MINS. WITH PAN COVERED WITH CIRCLE OF WAX PAPER.

REMOVE THE PAPER AND SPRINKLE GREENS WITH SALT AND PEPPER

ADD 4 CUPS WATER AND BRING TO BOIL

LOWER HEAT AND COOK 1 HOUR

PUREE SOUP IN A BLENDER – RETURN TO PAN

ADD CREAM AND LEMON JUICE

STIR WELL, HEAT AND SERVE OR CHILLL TWO HOURS AND SERVE COLD.

GREEN GARDENING BON APPETITE!

End of potages!

CHAPTER SEVEN

MY KINDS OF SALADS

When I say my kinds of salads, I say this because I have lived on salads for most of my adult life. For this reason I have developed a lot of variety, color, and utmost tastiness in the food I depended on for keeping slim when I was young. Now, at my age, salads are focused on health, vitality and weight Maintenance.

As far as healthy salads go, I am lucky because I loooove vegetables! It's sweets I am not addicted to. I actually have to force certain fruits (like pineapple for Bromeliad) on myself for health!

But salads were 60% of what I have called "meals" or "nourishment" for most of my life. Since I have done a program designed to set a goal of 75% raw food of total daily food intake; fruits and vegetables again have become; for new reasons, most of my total subsistence.

I love a tossed mixed vegetable salad anytime provided it is more than lettuce and tomatoes. The following accompaniments I use to make a salad more interesting, unless I have a terrible taste for my Mother-in-Laws old fashioned multi-vegetable salad with original Wish Bone Dressing. Then, it has to have the eight vegetables she used including not only lettuce (small cut chunks only) and tomato, but cucumbers, celery, carrots, radishes, green onion, as well as red onion. And, the vegetables have to be cut in the same little ½-inch-chunk-size-pieces she cut, otherwise it does not satisfy my taste for her salad when I am chewing or swallowing. And, as she did, it must be dressed only just before tossing and putting it on the table.

She also kept all the cut vegetables in separate cold water containers overnight until she actually tossed and dressed it. I have not gone this far these years even though I get yearnings to replicate her salad again! Somehow, the familiar chemicals in the Wish Bone bottle are enough (with the same cut size vegetable) to satisfy my memory or taste buds!

But, there are other vegetables when I am not making this old salad verbatim that can be added to any greens to spice and crunch flavors up a bit!

Beets	Artichoke Hearts (Canned)
Olives (Mostly black)	Hearts of Palm (Canned)
Zucchini (small tender garden chunks)	Chick Peas (Canned)

White or Green Asparagus Fresh Pea Pods

Broccoli

Broccoli Stalks (gently parboiled)

Green Beans (gently parboiled) Pimento (or chopped Green Olives

Butter Beans (Canned)

Any Greens, Kale, Romaine, Spinach	Bacon Bits (Spice Jar Variety)

Butter Crunch & Red & Boston Lettuces

Par Cooked Kohlrabi	Mushrooms of Any Kind

The following are salads I have taken to parties and gotten rave reviews on, so would like to share them with you:

GOURMET SPINACH SALAD

1 POUND MUSHROOMS (FRESH ONLY)
1 ONE POUND BAG SPINACH
3 HARD BOILED EGGS CHOPPED
½—1 LB. BACON COOKED & CRUMBLED

DRESSING

1 CUP SALAD OIL
½ CUP WINE VINEGAR
1 MEDIUM RED ONION CHOPPED
1 CUP SUGAR
1 TSP. WORCESTERSHIRE
2 TSP. SALT
YIELDS ENOUGH FOR 16

(CAN MAKE ½ FOR 8)

ASSEMBLE VEGETABLES AFTER BEING WASHED AND SPINACH SOAKED IN COLD WATER FOR AT LEAST 30 MINUTES. Rinse vegetables and toss with hard cooked egg and bacon just before ready to serve.

MIX INGREDIENTS FOR SALAD DRESSING WHILE VEGETABLES ARE SOAKING. SHAKE WELL AND REFRIGERATE AT LEAST 30 MINUTES.

ASSEMBLE SALAD AND DRESS. TOSS AND SERVE.

It's a classic and never fails to get comments and compliments and requests for recipes.

FIRE AND ICE GARDEN TOMATO SALAD

This is a salad that I take with me wherever I am invited in the summertime, Bar B Q's, House Parties, Wine Tasting, etc. It will go well with anything that is served and it's freshness alone carries it, and the way it is seasoned, like I carry it where ever we go.

8 GOOD SIZE GARDEN RIPE TOMATOES
CELERY SEED (1 TBLS.)
1 LARGE GREEN PEPPER
L RED ONION
1 LARGE OR 2 SMALL CUCUMBERS
GARLIC POWDER
6 CLOVES OF GARLIC
WINE VINEGAR & OIL TO TASTE

CUT TOMATOES IN HALVES AND THEN QUARTER OR EIGHTH HALVES SLICE CUCUMBER IN LARGE ROUNDS AND QUARTER THEM QUARTER RED ONION AND SEPARATE QUARTERED SLICES INTO LENGTHS. CUT GARLIC CLOVES INTO LONG SLICED THIN EIGHTS.

USE AT LEAST 1 TEASPOON TO 1 TABLESPOON OF GARLIC POWDER (THIS PROVIDES THE FIRE IN THE "FIRE & ICE")

MIX 3 TABLS. WINE VINEGAR WITH 1 – 2 TABLS. OIL

TO THIS MIXTURE I ADD WHATEVER FRESH BASIL, DILL, THYME, OR CHIVES I MAY HAVE IN MY HERB GARDEN. (OF COURSE, MUCH OF THIS IS TO TASTE. YOU MAY ALSO ADD A LITTLE DRY MUSTARD)

*THE EXTREME GARLIC IS WHAT MAKES THE "FIRE"

MIX ALL VEGETABLES AND CHILL A GOOD 2 HOURS—THE "ICE". MIX ONCE BEFORE SERVING.

TARRAGON THREE BEAN SALAD

I try to make this salad when I have fresh green beans in my garden, but it does not always work out that way. Easter season in Chicago does not yet produce fresh garden beans when I have a good spiral Ham to be complimented by this tasty combo. So I always keep canned on hand. But, on New Years' Day, I can always break down and buy them in the store fresh and cook them andante!

The bite of the tang of this salad will always scrumptiously compliment an entrée with it's "so right" combination of condiments!

1 CAN KIDNEY BEANS (ANY KIND)
1 CAN GREEN BEANS OR EQUIVALENT OF GARDEN VARIETY AFTER COOKING
1 CAN WAX BEANS
1 CAN CHICK PEAS (Optional or use for less carb content than kidney)
1 RED OR WHITE ONION (PREFERABLY RED)
1 STALK GREEN ONION
RED PIMENTO CHOPPED
¼ FRESH GREEN, RED, OR YELLOW BELL PEPPER CHOPPED
TARRAGON VINEGAR & VEGETABLE OIL
CELERY SEED (1 TABLS.)
ONION POWDER (1 TEAS.)
ANISE SEED (1 TEAS) OR SOME CHOPPED FRESH FENNEL

Mix together all ingredients except chopped, fresh, fennel, if used, and chill overnight. Trim with fennel when serving.

ESCAROLE (OR SPINACH) & BEANS WITH SAUSAGE

(CAN ALSO BE MADE WITHOUT SAUSAGE)
(Can double as a cold salad or hot or cold soup)

½ ONION
1 BUNCH ESCAROLE OR SPINACH GREENS
1 CAN CANNELINNI BEANS
1 LINK HOT OR MILD ITALIAN SAUSAGE SLICED THIN
3 SLICES MOZARELLA CHEESE
1 – 2 TABLS. ROMANO PRE-GRATED JARRED CHEESE

SAUTE SAUSAGE ROUNDS WITH ONION GENTLY. REMOVE
FROM PAN AND ADD WASHED AND DRYED ESCAROLE AND
SAUTE GENTLY AND BRIEFLY. (UNTIL A LITTLE BROWNED
BUT STILL SOMEWHAT CRISP).

TOSS ALL TOGETHER WITH BEANS, AND 2 CHEESES. SERVE
IN LARGE SALAD BOWL WITH GARLIC BREAD OR FRESH
ITALIAN BREAD OR BOTH ON SIDESS OF BOWL OR IN BREAD
BASKET.

If pairing with cup of soup, use stratichella made with greens used for
salad, in this case usually spinach but escarole is OK (with very little starch
added) as a compliment.

ELSIES' WALNUT, DRIED APRICOT PLATE WITH COTTAGE CHEESE, PEARS & HONEY/ MUSTARD DRESSING

* I add crumbled Feta or Low Fat Crumbled Blue Cheese all over the top of this.

My Aunt Elsie made this plate for me one day for lunch. It was a hot summer day and we had iced tea with the lunch. The flavors under the homemade honey/mustard whip are melded together to a perfection. Especially when my cheeses are crumbled over it.

I make it for my husband and I for supper on a hot summer's night when we are alone and serve it with cold or warm asparagus soup. It seems to go well with what seems to be an inconspicuous diet plate.

IT IS JUST AS WHAT APPEARS ABOVE IN THE TITLE LAYERED AROUND THE LOW FAT COTTAGE CHEESE ON THE PLATE, BUT IN THE END, SHE POURS WHIPPED (BY HAND) HONEY AND MUSTARD OVER IT!

Just copy this whole last paragraph above for entire recipe.

ARTICHOKE WITH BLACK OLIVE SALAD

1 CAN ARTICHOKE HEARTS WHOLE
1 CAN BLACK OLIVES PITTED
½ SMALL RED ONION SEAPARATED INTO SINGLE LENGHTS
RED WINE VINEGAR & OIL OR READY MADE RASPBERRY
VINAGRETTE DRESSING
MIX ABOVE AFTER QUARTERING ARTICHOKES AND CHILL
2 HOURS

I SOMETIMES ADD THINLY DICED SALAMI OR PEPPERONI
IF I HAVE IT!

This compliments any heavy Pasta Dish. If I am only serving Al Olio or Linguine with Clam Sauce, that is, something light in the cavalcade of Pasta Dishes, I may add the pepperoni or Hard Salami if I have it!

Nancy Dybek Greene

SOUR CREAM SALAD

The following is probably my favorite of all ensaladas. It is lunch, it is dinner, it is diet, it is existence and becomes the taste of delight. But there were many days when I made it as an entrée salad in summertime, for my family, or for myself if I happened to find myself to chill out and crunch my dinner. It is very satisfying and filling because of the Sour Cream, and some blue cheese or feta, if eaten while the Sour Cream has not watered down yet. IN other words, if eaten right after mixing.

1 boiled egg, cut on egg cutter and then quartered so pieces are small and will cover the bulk of the salad after mixing.
¼ head lettuce cut in small chunks
Red or Green onion, or white (if no other available) chopped or sliced thin
1 large tomato – quartered
1 – 2 slices any kind of cheese I have in the house, preferably blue or feta
(But any kind, even American will do)

Meat like ham or turkey or pepperoni, sliced in strips and then halved. About 2 slices.

Cucumber, quartered thick slices. About ½ cucumber.

Too much cucumber adds too much moisture and takes away the taste of a creamy Cobb salad that has been mixed with 4—8 ozs. sour cream. Enough to coat everything in the salad evenly.

Coarse ground pepper – at least 1/8 teaspoon
1/8 teaspoon Salt and a trace of celery salt.
1-8 oz. (if making for one person) or 1-16 oz. Sour cream

BROCCOLI SALAD

1 BUNCH BROCCOLI – CHOPPED
1 CUP RAISINS
1 CUP SUNFLOWER SEEDS
1 CUUP FINELY CHOPPED RED ONION
7 STRIPS CRISPY FRIED BACON (OR TURKEY BACON)

TOSS TOGETHER ABOVE INGREDIENTS

Chill (at least) 1 hour

Dress With:

1 CUP MANGO OR RASPBERRY VINAGRETTE DRESSING (FAT-FREE WORKS!)
½ CUP SUGAR
2 TABLS. LEMON JUICE

ASPARAGUS MOLDED SALAD

It is not Easter in my household without this salad! This, *I really mean! Literally!*

1 CAN ASPARAGUS SOUP (UNDILATED)
1 PKG. LIME JELLO
1 PKG.(8 OZ) CREAM CHEESE
½ CUP COLD WATER
½ CUP MAYO
¾ CUP CHOPPED CELERY
1 TABLS. GRATED ONION
½ CUP CHOPPED GREEN PEPPER
½ CUP CHOPPED PECANS

Heat Soup to boiling – Remove from heat – Add gelatin. Stir.—Add cheese & mix until melted – Add water. Heat until blended Stir in remaining ingredients. Oil mold (ring mold good, but Tupperware patterned molds— tulip, etc. also good, but more difficult to unmold)

Stir asparagus into mold after completely mixed.
Chill overnight and unmold carefully.

Note on unmolding: PLACE whole mold, once refrigerated overnight, into warm water bath for 10 minutes or so before turning over onto plate. If using Tupperware container remember to remove tulip preform from top before turning over onto flat plate.

I usually use a ring mold for this or my tomato aspic to avoid problems unmolding.

Refrigerate again for at least ½ hour or so before serving immediately after unmolding.

The crunchiness of this mold makes it unusual with it's unsweet, vegetable taste. It is a pure Easter winner, in color and uniqueness in taste.

TANGY TOMATO RING

I have made many classics aspics because I am not basically a sweet lover and prefer a vegetable taste to a meal accompaniment, but they are time consuming for the most part. This ring is quick and good and satisfies an undeniable urge or yearning for aspic more than the classic version. I have added ingredients to it through the years and I am proud of my evolved rendition!

Combine 21/2 cups, V-8 vegetable juice, one 6 oz. Can tomato paste, 2 tablespoons tarragon vinegar, 1 cup minced onion, 1 tablespoon finely chopped green pepper, 1 teaspoon, salt, dash pepper, and 1 bay leaf.

Bring to boil. Soften 2 envelopes unflavored gelatin, in 1.2 cup cold water; add to hot mixture. Add ¾ teaspoon grated lemon peel, 1 ½ tablespoons lemon juice, and ¼ teaspoon basil; stir well. Remove bay leaf.

Pour into 5-cup ring mold. Chill firm. Unmold on greens. If desired, fill center with crab meat or tuna. Pass ranch dressing.

Crab Meat Version: Chill aspic until partially set. Add on 6 ½ or 7 ½ oz crab meat flaked and 4 stuffed green olives sliced with 3 tablespoons anchovy paste. Pour into mold and chill firm. This can be an entrée during lent served with Clam Chowder or Crab Bisque.

CHAPTERS Eight & Nine

MY FAVORITE MEALS

As in the Christmas song "these are a few of my favorite things," my favorite meals are sometimes associated with holidays but most of them are made continuously as well as seasonally.

My Pepper Steak has probably been my family's all time favorite, but I know they enjoy it more when the tomatoes and green peppers and onions and celery are fresh from the garden. However, when I serve it with giant popovers from the oven in the dead of winter, this tantalizing distracting accompaniment overcomes the taste of store bought produce!

My husband's favorite besides the above is Roasted Capon with dressing or Roasted Cornish Hens with wild rice. Either of these will make him come home early on any day. As well as a good spaghetti dinner with homemade Meatballs and Italian Sausage in the Sauce and Garlic Bread made with fresh Italian Bread (also put in the bread basket as fresh bread to be spread with butter in between crunches of Garlic Bread). With my great Artichoke and Black Olive Salad, it's a feast for a King!

My meals for a week are more often organized by Meat economics, or what is on sale in local grocery stores as well as what my week looks like in terms of heavy work schedule and often the weather or season. And then, there's the soup factor: If I make a pot of soup every week except in the summer time, the kind of soup I make may affect what type of meals I produce during that week. If I make the Chicken Soup, the likelihood of my making a Chicken Dinner on a day outside of the day I make Chicken Soup, is not too likely!

But I like to sort out my meals in categories in this writing. So I will start with Chicken, since it is the most used category of all foods, whether it be for soup, meals, salads, dieting or just because, if you have any kind of food appreciation like my husband, he would be happy with eating Chicken every other day! Or more!

And, being that this cookbook is based on Economy, Chicken is a main subject here, for sure. I buy legs and thighs on sale and store them in little packages (of four legs and thighs). Then, at the whim of a moment, I can make soup or a quick Chicken and rice dish or Chicken Chow Mien, or any or many quick Chicken recipes that are in my 30 minute recipe file.

I must also buy whole Chickens when they are on sale and stack them on one corner of my freezer in order of time; purchased with newer ones on the bottom going older to the top. When I make good Roasted Chicken that takes a little time on a day when I am going to be home and can watch them just by smelling their stages, I want whole Chickens! I stuff them with various themes of what we have a taste for, like wild rice after too much holiday dressing, etc. or vegetables if we are being diet conscious or health conscious or garden conscious, (if not using my garden vegetables is making me feel guilty).

Here, I start with the easiest of delectable Chicken Dishes and go to the more complicated!

CHICKEN WITH RICE

3 – 4 POUNDS FRYING CHICKEN, CUT IN PIECES
1/3 CUP SEASONED FLOUR
¼ CUP BUTTER
1 CUP CREAM OF CHICKEN SOUP
2 ½ TBLS. GRATED ONION
1 TSP. SALT
DASH PEPPER
1 TBLS. CHOPPED PARSLEY
½ TSP. CELERY FLAKES
1/3 TSP. THYME
1 1/3 CUPS WATER
1 1/3 CUPS RICE

ROLL 6 – 8 PIECES CHICKEN IN 1/3 CUP SEASONED FLOUR.
BROWN CHICKEN PIECES IN BUTTER.

COOK SOUP AND WATER & STIR TO A BOIL. SPREAD MINUTE
RICE (RIGHT FROM BOX) IN 1 ¾ QUART SHALLOW CASSEROLE.
POUR ALL BUT 1/3 CUP SOUP OVER RICE, STIR TO MOISTEN.
TOP WITH CHICKEN AND REST OF SOUP. BAKE, COVERED,
AT 375 FOR 30 MINUTES OR UNTIL TENDER. GARNISH WITH
PAPRIKA. MAKES 4 – 6 SERVINGS

Bake Chicken for 45 minutes or until Chicken is done and juices of
Chicken are immersed into rice.

This can be fancied up with any kind of sautéed onion, garlic, green
pepper, leek, mushrooms or any available vegetables added sautéed before
browning chicken or adding to rice mixture before baking with Soup
poured over.

This is always really scrumptious and easy if you are busy and can even
be made without browning the Chicken if you don't have time to watch
it. In this case, leave it in the oven for fifteen minutes longer or so or until
Chicken is brown and rice is cooked between chicken drippings and soup.

My favorite way to prepare this is to add sautéed onion, garlic, red pepper and a small can of mushrooms to the rice mixture before I pour over the soup and top it with the Chicken pieces. I have also put pineapple pieces, and green pepper pieces over this, instead of the artichokes, and Asian Sweet and Sour Dressing instead of Ranch Dressing, before baking, to make it taste like Sweet and Sour Chicken when the flavors melded. A sprinkle of soy sauce over the whole mixture before baking and your family will be amazed! 45 Minute Dinner Wonders never cease!

SUPER EASY CHICKEN
WITH ARTICHOKE DELIGHT

1 BOTTLE RANCH DRESSING
1 JAR ARTICHOKE HEARTS (MARINATED)
½ 16 OZ PACKAGE COOKED NOODLES
4 – 6 BAKED CHICKEN BREASTS

PLACE CHICKEN BREASTS OVER BED OF COOKED NOODLES
POUR OVER ARTICHOKE HEARTS AND TOP WITH RANCH
DRESSING, EVENLY SPREADING OVER ALL INGREDIENTS IN
9 X 13 GLASS BAKING DISH OR EQUIVALENT BAKING DISH

BAKE FOR 20 – 25 MINUTES
30 MINUTE EASY BREEZY CHICKEN MARSALA

1 – 1 ½ CUP MARSALA WINE (NOT COOKING WINE)
1 CUP CHICKEN BROTH
4 – 6 CHICKEN TENDERS OR BREASTS CUT IN HALVES
1 CUP SEASONED FLOUR (ADD SALT, PEPPER TO FLOUR) (OR
ADD SEASONED SALT TO FLOUR)

FLOUR CHICKEN PIECES AND SHAKE OFF EXCESS FLOUR

SAUTE 5 SHALLOTS OR GARLIC CLOVES IN OLIVE OIL (3
TBLS. AND BUTTER (3 TBLS) REMOVE.

SAUTE CHICKEN 1 MINUTE ON EACH SIDE IN SHALLOT
DRIPPINGS

REMOVE CHICKEN

SAUTE 1—2 CUP MUSHROOMS (FRESH IF POSSIBLE) IN
SHALLLOTS & CHICKEN DRIPPINGS

ADD 1 CUP MARSALA WINE & 1 CUP CHICKEN BROTH

ADD CHICKEN AGAIN

COOK IN PAN TOGETHER 10 MINUTES OR UNTIL CHICKEN DONE.

POUR OVER PASTA, RICE, NOODLES OR MASHED POTATOES

DOUBLE PARMESAN CHICKEN BREASTS

4—6 CHICKEN BREASTS POUNDED OUT
FLOUR AND PARMESAN CHICKEN PIECES

DIP IN WHISKED EGG BATTER WITH FRESH CUT UP CHIVES

RE-FLOUR WITH PARMESAN (IF POSSIBLE USE PARMESAN OF
GREATER GRANULES OR SHREDDED BY HAND)

BAKE IN OVEN FOR 30 MINUTES

REAL SPANISH CHICKEN

CORIANDER 1 TSP.
GROUND CLOVES 1 TSP. SPICES
CINNAMON 1 TSP.
CUMIN ½ TSP.

VEGETABLES

CELERY 2 STALKS
1 SMALL ONION
2 CLOVES GARLIC
ANCHO PEPPER BROTH MIXED WITH CHICKEN BROTH

(BOILE 4 ANCHO PEPPERS FOR 10-15 MINUTES

SAUTE FIRST FOUR VEGETABLES IN BUTTER OR MARGARINE

COMBINE ALL INGREDIENTS IN OSTERIZER AND POUR OVER CHICKEN BREASTS

(Real Spanish Chicken continued)

Bake 35 –40 MINUTES

SERVE WITH RICE & FRIOLES

EASY CHICKEN PAPRIKASH

¼ CUP FLOUR
1 TSP. SALT
3-4 TBSP PAPRIKA ADD 3-4 MORE AFTER CHICKEN PREPARED
¼ TSP PEPPER
1 FRYER/BROILER CHICKEN OR EQUIVALENT
2 ½—3 LBS. OR SMALL CHICKENS HALVED FOR 1 TO EACH
PERSON SERVING

PAPRIKASH GRAVY

4 TBLS. MORE PAPARIKA
½ STICK BUTTER
¼ CUP SLICED GREEN ONION
1 CAN CREAM OF CHICKEN SOUP
1 CUP SOUR CREAM
1 CUP FRESH OR CANNED MUSROOMS

IN BOWL, COMBINE FLOUR, SALT, PAPRIKA AND PEPPER, AND COAT CHICEKEN WITH FLOUR MIXTURE. IN SKILLET, SAUTE UNTIL TENDER AND LIGHTLY BROWNED. REMOVE CHICKEN TO SERVING PLATTER, KEEP WARM. ADD 3 MORE TBLS. PAPRIKA. STIR. INTO GRAVY. WARM GENTLY BUT DO NOT BOIL. LOWER CHICKEN INTO GRAVY AND COOK 10 MINUTES BEFORE ADDING SOUR CREAM TO MIXTURE.

BEST EVER HERB ROASTED CHICKEN

2 WHOLE CHICKEN OR CAPON
BUTTER (ENOUGH TO SPREAD OVER CHICKENS
GENEROUSLY BY HOLDING BUTTER ON STICK) PROBABLY
LESS THAN 1 STICK
DIJON MUSTARD ¼ CUP
ROSEMARY
TYME
BLACK PEPPER COARSE GROUND
GARLIC POWDER
COARSE GROUND SALT
SEASONED SALT

BUTTER BOTH CHICKENS WITH STICK BUTTTER, INSIDE AND OUT. RUB WITH DIJON MUSTARD. SALT INSIDE OF CHICKENS WITH COARSE GROUND SALT AND PEPPER.

STUFFF WITH DESIRED STUFFING – CELERY BUTTER OR WILD RICE!

SPRINKLE ALL OTHER SPICES ON OUTER SKIN OF CHICKENS.

ROAST AT 400 DEGREES FOR 10-12 MINUTES OR UNTIL STARTING TO BROWN.

REDUCE OVEN TO 325 FOR 1 ½ HOURS IF CHICKEN IS STUFFED.

PUT POTATOES, SQUASHES, OR OTHER VEGETABLES THAT TASTE GOOD AFTER BEING BAKE INTO OVEN WHILE CHICKENS ROAST. HOUSE WILL SMELL EVEN BETTER THAN ROASTED CHICKEN!

QUICK ROASTED CHICKEN

IN OMELET TYPE COATED FRY PAN, SAUTE CHICKEN ON BOTH SIDES ON HIGH FLAME AFTER SEASONING & COATING WITH MUSTARD & MAPLE SYRUP MIXED (WITH HANDS).

PUT INTO COVERED ROASTING PAN OR ANY PAN COVERED WITH TIN FOIL AFTER SPRINKLING WITH DESIRED HERBS AS IN "BEST-EVER" RECIPE OR JUST USE LAWRY'S SEASONED SALT.

ROAST 1 HOUR WITH PARTIALLY PEELED SMALL POTATOES AND ONIONS SURROUNDING BIRD.

TURN VEGETABLES AROUND BIRD 3 TO 4 TIMES WHILE ROASTING.

SERVE CHICKEN SURROUNDED WITH ROASTED VEGETABLE.

EASY "FROM SCRATCH" CHICKEN KIEV

8 CHICKEN BREASTS
BUTTER OR FLEISCHMANN'S MARGARINE

POUND OUT BONED CHICKEN BREASTS VERY THIN,. PLACE 1/1/2 TBSP. MARGARINE OR BUTTTER IN CENTER OF EACH SPREADING OVER BREAST WITH BUTTER KNIFE.

COMBINE 4 TBSP CHIVES, (FRESH) 1 TSP. SALT AND 1/8 TSP. PEPPER, SPRINKLE OVER MARGARINE OR BUTTER. BEAT 4 EGG WHITES AND 2 TBSP MILK TOGETHER. ROLL CHICKEN IN BREAD CRUMBS, THEN IN EGG WHITE MIXTURE AND AGAIN IN BREAD CRUMBS, COAT WELL. Refrigerate at least 20 minutes. Fry in hot vegetable oil until well browned 8 – 10 minutes. Drain well. Serve hot. Makes 8 servings over cooked rice.

CHICKEN IN THE POT

1 CAST IRON DUTCH OVEN
1 WHOLE CHICKEN
1 WHOLE TURNIP OR SQUASH
6 WHOLE POTATOES

BROWN CHICKEN WHOLE TURNING IN HOT VEGETABLE OIL IN CAST IRON POT AFTER SEASONING WITH SALT, PEPPER, AND GARLIC POWDER. ADD WHOLE POTATOES AND ANY OTHER DESIRED VEGETABLE THAT WILL TAKE 40 MINUTES OR SO TO COOK. ADD ½ TO 1 CUP WATER.

COVER WITH CAST IRON LID. COOK UNTIL TENDER AND VEGETABLES COMPLETE.

*I USE THIS SAME METHOD TO COOK LAMB SHANK BUT USUALLY ADD RICE MIXED WITH CHOPPED ONION INSTEAD OF THE ABOVE VEGETABLES. THEY, THE LAMB AND THE CHICKEN IS SCRUMPTIOUS THIS WAY.

CHICKEN PICCATA

4 GOOD SIZE CHICKEN BREASTS CUT IN SCALLOPINE STRIPS (ABOUT 10 PCs)

LIGHTLY FLOUR WITH SEASONED FLOUR.

REMOVE FROM PAN

SAUTE GARLIC – 6 CLOVES

SQUEEZE JUICE OF ONE WHOLE LEMON INTO PAN

ADD 10 OLIVES

ADD ¼ TO ½ CUP CAPERS

ADD 1 CUP WHITE WINE

ADD 2 CUPS CHICKEN BROTH

SLICE SQUEEZED LEMON INTO SLICES AND ADD TO MIXTURE

MAY THICKEN MIXTURE WITH CORNSTARCH & WATER

RE-ADD CHICKEN SCALLOPINE SLICES

SERVE OVER FETTUCINE, LEMON SLICES AND ALL!

BEEF DISHES

Assuming that everyone has their own way of knowing how they like their Steaks raw 0or burnt, I have only included here my exclusive Beef recipes that are not known to everyone and worth, I think (and my family) for mentioning. This book is to help a cook to enhance what they already know about cooking, not to teach anyone how to cook and time roasts or steaks. Therefore, these are not only specialty recipes, tried and tested by me for years rather than new and innovative cooking trends that are focused on marketing well. That is, they are proposed to be made based on budget cooking and fresh foods at daily market prices. A practice that can enhance cooking with the vitality of less expensive ingredients, consistently. An expensive steak can always be enjoyed at home when on sale at the market, or in a restaurant anytime or for a special occasion. However, I must say a few words about what I do with a Steak to make it taste like restaurant quality at the end of this chapter.

The following are favorites of mine and do not have to be expensive to be absolutely, out-of-this-world-ambrosial!

Nancy Dybek Greene

HUNGARIAN BEEF GOULASH

2 TABLS. BUTTER
1 – 2 LBS BONELESS BEEF CHUCK
CUT INTO 1 IN. PIECES
1 LB. ONIONS PEELED AND SLICED
2-3 TABLS. ALL PURPOSE FLOUR
2-3 TABLS. PAPRIKA
1 LB. SWEET RED PEPPERS
(3 ½ CUPS) SEEDED AND CUT INSTRIPS
1 CUP CANNED TOMATOES WITH THEIR JUICE
1/1/2 TSP. SALT
½ TEAS. GROUND PEPPER
2 CUPS WATER

FLOUR, SALT AND PEPPER CHUCK PIECES ON HIGH HEAT IN DUTCH OVEN 2 MINUTES. STIR IN ONIONS, REDUCE HEAT, STIRRING 5 MINUTES UNTIL ONIONS ARE GOLDEN, NOT BROWN. SPRINKLE FLOUR AND PAPRIKA OVER ONIONS AND STIR UNTIL MOISTENED. ADD REMAINING INGREDIENTS, AND BRING TO A BOIL OVER HIGH HEAT, THEN REDUCE AND SIMMER. STIR. COVER & SIMMER 2 HOURS, UNTIL MEAT IS VERY TENDER. Makes 5 cups Hungarian Goulash. Reheat well. Can serve over noodles, rice or mashed potatoes.

220 calories
20 grams fat
21 grams carbohydrates

BEEF BIRDS—PTACKY (ROMUPS)
(Romups - Short for Roll Em Ups)

This next meaty dish, involves a little work, is very old world, but is really easy, time wise, and the flavor combinations will addict any cook to making it several times, probably during the winter. You can alternate home made noodles (end of this chapter) rice, finger dumplings or just a side vegetable that takes gravy well, like mashed potatoes.

2-3 LB. ROUND STEAK or 6 cube steaks
¼ CUP REGULAR MUSTARD
DILL PICKLE – 6 SLICES
QUARTER SLICED ONION SLICES (WEDGES)

CUT MEAT INTO SERVING SIZE PIECES (LIKE 2 X 2 IN. SQUARES

POUNG MEAT OUT IN INDIVIDUAL PIECES DUSTING WITH SEASONED FLOUR AND TURNING AND POUNDING ON BOTH SIDES UNTIL SQUARE ARE ALMOST DOUBLED IN SIZE.

SPREAD MUSTARD OVER EACH SERVINGS PIECE

LAY PICKLE ACROSS EACH SLICE LENGHTWISE

ADD ONION

ROLL MEAT UP COVERING VEGETABLE

TOOTHPICK EACH "BIRD" TO PREPARE FOR SAUTEING

SAUTE EACH IN GARLIC BUTTER OR MARGARINE

UNTIL BROWN.

POUR 1 CUP WATER INTO SAUTE PAN, COVER AND SIMMER ON VERY LOW HEAT FOR 40 MINUTES, ADDING WATER AS NEEDED.

WHEN MEAT IS TENDER, REMOVE PIECES, ADD ANOTHER ¼ CUP MUSTARD TO LIQUID IN PAN WITH ½ CUP PICKLE JUICE. SEASON WITH SALT AND PEPPER TO TASTE, THEN THICKEN WITH CORNSTARCH AND WATER UNTIL A LIGHT, YELLOW CREAMY GRAVY APPEARS.

ADD MEAT AND SERVE OVER RICE, NOODLES, MASHED POTATOES OR CARBOHYDRATE FREE MASHED CAULIFLOWER.

BEEF STROGANOFF

1 ½ LB. SIRLOIN OR ROUND
3 TBS. BUTTER
1 CUP SLICED IN ½ OR WHOLE FRESH MUSHROOMS
1 LB. ONION SLICE
2 CUPS BEEF BOULLION OR CONSIMME
2 TABLS. FLOUR
2 TABLS. TOM PASTE (I USE KETCHUP RATHER THAN WASTE
A WHOLE CAN OF TOM. PASTE)
1 TSP,. MUSTARD
2/3 – CUP SOUR CREAM
3 TABLS. SHERRY OR ANY DRY WINE.

REMOVE ALL FAT, CUT INTO NARROW STRIPS ABOUT 2 ½
LONG X ¾ WIDE AND ¼ TO ½ " THICK. Dust strips with salt &
pepper or tenderizer & set aside 2 hours at room temp. When ready, melt
3 tbls. Butter in skillet and sauté 3 mushrooms until tender (about 5 min).
Remove and in same butter sauté onion until brown remove. Add about 1
tbls. Butter & when bubbling hot, sear strips of beef on all sides but leave
rare. Remove. To butter in skillet add 1 tabls. flour blend and brown. Then
slowly, while stirring add 2 cup bouillon to make smooth gravy. Next add
win, tom. Paste & mustard. Add vegetables and meat. Simmer 20 min. 5
minutes before serving add sour cream & blend just to heat. Do not boil
once 2/3 cup sour cream is added . . . (1 cup better)

Serve over rice, noodles, or whipped potatoes.

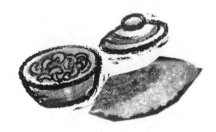

PEPPER STEAK

1 lb. Beef Chuck, cut in very thin strips
¼ cup cooking (vegetable) oil
1 clove garlic, minced
1 tbsp. Soy sauce
1 tsp. Salt
¼ cup water
1 cup green pepper, cut in 1" pieces
1 cup chopped onion
1 cup chopped celery
1/1 to 16 oz. Fresh mushrooms or 2 small cans
1 tbsp. Cornstarch
1 cup water
4 Beef Bouillon Cubes (should not need more if beef well browned)
2 tomatoes, cut in eighths

Brown beef in hot oil; add garlic and cook until yellow. Add soy sauce, salt and ¼ cup water; cook 45 min. Add vegetables; cook 10 min. Stir in cornstarch blended with 1 cup water; add tomatoes and cook 5 min. Serve over hot fluffy rice, 4 servings.

I usually use round steak; it works out best for this recipe. I dredge it in seasoned flour on both sides and briefly tenderizer with a wooden mallet.

Sometimes, I just start out with cubed steak instead of round steak and then I can skip this step and season the cubed steaks with salt and pepper or Lawry's seasoned salt. I brown the meat, (whatever you may use) really well, so that it may provide a good brown gravy for the end result. When I cook the meat, I sometimes add water and cook it as long as it takes to make the meat tender. At the end of this step, I have only the skeleton of what is to complete the tantalizing and satisfying end result.

After I add the vegetables, (except for the tomatoes which are added only at the end) I add about a ½ cup of dark, dry wine like burgundy or Chianti, but Merlot or sauvignon cabernet work fine also. At this step, I also thicken the gravy with cornstarch mixture which usually takes, (for the amount I make) about 3 tbls. Of cornstarch to one cup water. After the wine and cornstarch mixture, I add the tomatoes last, just before the presentation so they don't cook down into the gravy, and hold a nice contrast to the green peppers in the pot. I also use whole black peppers, about 12 or so.

ALTERNATION ON RECIPE: Make pepper steak gravy without meat or for that matter with meat, but very little and pour over broiled steaks. Nice way to vary this recipe for a romantic dinner for two or a special company dinner for 4 to 6 people. Grate fresh black pepper over steaks before broiling.

TO ACCOMPANY MEAT DISHES

HOME MADE NOODLES

This is a recipe I have used for about 40 years. It never fails to impress people, as humble as it is. Sometimes I have used this same dough for pierogies or raviolis and it has worked just as well for them.

It is a very simple noodle dough and can be used in soups as egg drops. But the savory flavor and consistency of the hand rolled and kitchen table dried noodles are at it's best buttered and under some wonderful meat dish like those in this chapter. I roll out my noodles while I am waiting for my meat dishes to simmer. Let them dry for 20 minutes before cutting with a pastry wheel, and then again dry after cutting for at least one hour. I quickly boil them only after my meat dishes are ready. These wonderful noodles are a real compliment to any meat dish presentation, are quick and easy. And, you can make them as thin or thick as you like to eat them.

Combine 1 beaten egg, ½ teaspoon salt, and 2 tabls. milk; add 1 cup sifted all purpose flour or enough to make stiff dough. Roll very thin on floured surface; let stand 20 minutes. Roll up loosely; slice ½ inch wide, unroll, spread out and let dry 1—2 hours.

Drop into boiling soup or boiling, salted water, and cook uncovered about 10 minutes.

Makes 3 cups cooked noodles.

STEAK BROILING

A lot of learning about cooking took place in my life while watching chefs in the fine dining restaurants I worked in. They did things that my Mother did not know about cooking or no cook book ever could teach me.

First of all, all fine-dining restaurants usually started with Choice Meat. At least, this was always my experience. If people ordered their Steak Well Done, (always a bad choice) we had to warn customers that well done may ruin or toughen the steak.

Chef's season steaks before they broil your order with Seasoned Salt, and always pour melted butter over them right after they are broiled. When you serve them and people make comments like "Oh! It tastes like butter!" or "Oh, it cuts and tastes just like butter" it's because there is butter over it and to begin with it is a good quality of meat.

So, whenever I know I am going to be broiling steak, I let them sit out at room temperature with a seasoned Meat Tenderizer on them (since those I buy are not always Choice) and after forking them a little, I dab a little warm water on them, or drop it over with a spoon. Then I use the seasoned salt and let them sit at room temperature for an hour or so tenderizing them. Note: I always buy the thickest steaks I can buy in a store, because it increases the promise of them coming out medium rare under a home broiler. I also pour butter over them immediately before serving them. My melted butter has a small drop of Worcestershire and some mushrooms whether pre-cooked fresh mushrooms, or canned.

RIB ROAST OR ANY ROAST

Before putting the thermometer in a roast, raise the temperature of the Oven Up to about 500 degrees and insert roast for about half hour. After 30 or 40 minutes have passed, depending on size of roast, turn the temperature down to get the natural juices to come from the top fat of the Roast. When the chef will turn the roast down to the temperature at which it should be roasted, these juices will rally from the high heat of the meat and make a tender but crusty and delicious outer layer from which the whole roast takes flavor. Usually the outer layer is covered with black coarse ground pepper, coarse ground sea salt, or if it is Pork these plus Caraway seed. To these kinds of seasonings on the outer surface of a roast can be added garlic powder, fresh garlic or seasoned salt. I happen to like all of the above when I make a Standing Rib Roast and the crust that forms on the outer layer of Roast after the half hour or so of the elevated 500 degree temperature!

LAMB AND VEAL

Lamb is my favorite of all meals, but usually quite expensive. Veal is not as delicious to me, but even more expensive and must be delicately prepared in order to get one's money's worth.

I use Roast Leg of Lamb to mark the holiday of Easter and the coming of Spring. Aside from that lamb entrée, I have only one great lamb dish which does not cost an "arm and a leg" and is great! A good roasting leg, with some fresh garlic, course salt and black pepper crusting is unlikely to be anything but scrumptious. It seems like it's more affordable in Spring, even if it is the only time I can afford it – for Easter. In many cultures, it is a religious symbol, so it serves a double purpose, and another good reason to spend money to celebrate Spring. You can get roasted lamb on Sundays in many restaurants, or at an Easter brunch. However, no restaurant lamb compares with the lamb from my own oven on Easter Sunday with it's crusty bits and pieces that come off of the encrusted with seasoning, top of the leg. This would be hours after we have consumed scrambled eggs with Polish Sausage cut into it, and Houska, our Polish yellow Easter bread, sometimes known as Twist (braided for Easter).

LAMB SHANKS

4 ½ pound Lamb Shanks
Mixed fresh soup vegetables like, celery, onion, carrots.
Garlic Powder

Rub Garlic Powder on Shanks

Brown Lamb Shanks in Cast Iron Dutch Oven on semi-high flame. Or Regular Pot that has fitting cover. Pour in about 1 quart of water over very brown shanks. Add vegetables.

Simmer until tender – about 2 or more hours.

Add 1 Cup Rice last 30 minutes or more.

Rice will thicken gravy. I serve this dish as is straight from the pot onto serving dish with mint jelly on the side. The starch and vegetables are already in the dish.

VEAL

The only veal roast I have ever ventured was Veal Pocket since it is proclaimed to be low in price. It was delicious because of the way I seasoned it and the dressing inside the pocket, but stuffed Chicken would have probably tasted just as well or even better. And, the veal pocket was not really that cheap, but I did it because it was on our Sunday, special menu in the restaurant where I worked, and drew a lot of customers since it was the only place that offered this old Bohemian (Czech) dish.

I have repeatedly made two veal dishes all of my life, one, a kind of peasant dish that often is made with chicken instead of veal, the other, an absolutely delectable scaloppini that enhances the taste of veal more than any other recipe I have ever encountered. I don't make Wienerschnitzel, since I try not to eat fried meat, and I can order it in many Chicago restaurants.

Nancy Dybek Greene

VEAL A'LA'MADELON

1 CLOVE GARLIC
2 LB. BONELESS VEAL, CUT IN BITE-SIZE PIECES
2 TBSP. FLOUR
1 TSP. SALT
¼ TSP. PEPPER
TWO 1" WIDE STRIPS LEMON PEEL
1 CUP BOILING WATER
1 CUP HEAVY CREAM

Sauté garlic in hot butter in heavy skillet. Remove garlic and brown veal in the butter. Sprinkle flour, salt, and pepper over meat. Brown again. Add lemon peel and water. Cover. Simmer about 1 hr. until tender. Remove lemon peel. Stir in cream. Heat through. Serve hot over parsley buttered Potatoes. 4 to 6 servings.

PARSLEY BUTTERED NEW SPRING POTATOES

Semi-peel 8-10 new red spring potatoes.

Cut in half, boil and toss when andante with butter and parsley and chives.

If fresh not available, a 1 lb. Can of small whole potatoes is just right for four when cut in half and tossed warm with butter, parsley and chives. Sans the chives for tips of green onion or just parsley and butter may suffice.

VEAL SCALLOPINE

4 slices veal shoulder chop or round bone chop
½ CUP All purpose flour
Salt,Pepper & Paprika
1-2 6 oz. Cans Mushrooms
1 Bouillon Cube
1—Cup 8 oz. Can Tomato Sauce
¼ Cup Chopped Green Pepper
1 8 oz. Package Tagliatelle Verdi (Green Noodles)

Pound meat thoroughly with meat pounder. Cut in serving pieces. Season flour with 1 teaspoon salt, dash pepper, and 2 teaspoons paprika. Coat meat in mixture. Brown in hot fat. Place in 13x9x2 inch baking dish.

Drain mushrooms, reserving liquid. Add water to mushroom liquid to make 1 cup heat to boiling. Dissolve bouillon cube in the hot liquid and pour over meat.

Bake in moderate oven (350) 30 minutes. Combine tomato sauce, green pepper, and mushrooms, pour over the meat and continue baking for 15 minutes more. Meanwhile, cook noodles until tender in boiling salted water; drain. Baste meat with the sauce just before serving. Sprinkle with Parmesan cheese. Serve with hot buttered noodles. Makes 4 servings.

CHAPTER TEN

WHEN THE CHANGE IS LOW

The best of concoctions are invented from the TITLE above. Except my Bohemian Pizza. This, I copied from Chef Stella Umlauf, of Café Europe. Everyday the teachers who came in from the local Public School ordered this. And, I mean, everyday of the year . . . . . with a cup of soup. The lettuce and tomato that were served as a garnish, they used as salad, pouring dressing from a lazy Susan Stella laid out in the morning to save the waitresses time dressing salads. One less chore to worry about during the panic and mayhem of lunch.

There was a certain taste to Her's that is hard for me to duplicate, because she always used real bacon, and I seldom do. I use precooked bacon or bacon bits, to keep this an easy, breezy little lunch treat.

Anyway, for a Czech restaurant, she sold more of this item than Roast Duck and Kneliky or Zeli. (Dumplings and Sauerkraut) Truth is always stranger than fiction, even in cooking.

So the following not only sustained a low budget month, or period of waiting for a paycheck, but also were preferred items in a restaurant with fine dining.

BOHEMIAN PIZZA

2 slices white bread toasted (Stella broiled them and then added the next
    ingredients)
2 – 3 slices American Cheese
2-3 Tomato Slices
Bacon bits, about ¼ cup per sandwich
Melted butter

Toast bread with a little of the melted butter on the broiler (like Stella) or
toast bread in the toaster and butter after toasted.

Assemble Sandwiches
Place Tomato slices over toasted bread
Place cheese singles over tomato (I use 1 and ½ slices on each piece).
Sprinkle with bacon bits or crumbled precooked or regular bacon.
Spoon a little of the melted butter over each loaded slice.
Broil, not right under fire, but lower so cheese doesn't burn while melting.

(About 1 and ½ minutes)

Remove from Oven and Cut into 4 diagonals.
Serve in diagonals along the length of plate.

If you make this for a group, it is better to give each person an individual
plate with the above served on it than to serve it on a large platter like
pizza. It goes further because, when people are served their own plate
and finish, they are usually embarrassed to ask for more. It is enough! My
children always wanted it served like pizza so they could eat more, but
once finishing the 2 slices cut into 4 diagonals, they never asked for more!

SPAGHETTI PIE

6 oz. Spaghetti 1 cup tom. paste
2 tbls. Butter 1 tsp. Sugar
1/3 cup parmesan cheese 1 tsp. Oregano
2 Eggs, beaten ½ teas. Garlic salt
½ lb. Ground beef 1 cup small curd creamed cottage cheese
½ cup onion chopped 1 cup mozzarella cheese shredded
1/2 cup onion chopped
¼ cup green pepper

Cook spaghetti according to pkg. Drain & put in bowl (3 ¼ cups spaghetti). Stir butter in spaghetti then stir in parmesan cheeses & eggs. Form spaghetti into a crust in a greased oversized pie plate & set aside.

Cook meat, brown and add onion & green pepper to tender, until meat is browned. Drain fat. Stir in tomatoes, paste, sugar, oregano & garlic. Heat thoroughly. Spread cottage cheese over spaghetti crust. Fill pie with meat & tomato mixture.

Bake uncovered in 350 oven for 20 minutes. Take out of oven and sprinkle mozzarella cheese on top. Bake 5 min. longer or until cheese melts.

HAM/POTATOE CASSEROLE

2 BOXES AU GRATIN POTATOE MIX
LEFT OVER HAM – CUT INTO PIECES THIN AS YOU CAN

FOLLOW DIRECTIONS ON AUGRATIN PACKAGES
INTERJECT PIECES OF HAM INTO POTATOI MIX
ABOUT 1 CUP OR – NO MORE
BAKE AS DIRECTED!

SALMON LOAF

1 CAM 16 OZ. ANY KIND OF SALMON

½ Teaspoon each of the following:

ONION SALT
GARLIC SALT
BLACK COARSE GROUND PEPPER
CELERY SEED
MUSTAR SEED
¼ TEAS. CRUSHED RED PEPPER
¼ Cup lemon juice
1 Beaten Egg
2 Green Onions

Mix and Bake in Loaf Pan at 3:50 for 30-40 Minutes

SALMON PATTIES

Form above mixture into patties and sauté in vegetable oil.

Make white sauce and pour over when serving.
I serve mine usually with a package of frozen pierogies I've been hiding in the freezer just for these short-times.

White sauce: MEDIUM Makes 1 cup
2 tbls. Butter or margarine
2 tbls. All-purpose flour
1/4 teas. Salt
1 cup milk

Melt butter in saucepan over low heat. Blend in flour, salt, and dash white pepper. Add milk all at once. Cook quickly, stirring constantly, till mixture thickens and bubbles,—wooden spoon is good. Pour over your entrée of choice.

LIVER & ONIONS

Soak 1 pound beef liver in milk for 1 hour.
Shake in seasoned bag of flour, 1 piece at a time.
Sauté 1 minute on each side in margarine in non-stick pan.

Liver should have a light, golden brown coating. At this point, it will be rare inside.

If you like it done more than this, than do no more than 1/1/2 minute on each side or it will be the shoe leather liver I ate all of my childhood. Also, soaking it in milk will make it taste like milk-fed calf's liver. I serve this with a white sauce that has sugar and vinegar in it, sort of sweet/sour. It is extremely enhancing to a strong flavor like liver and can also be poured over mashed potatoes or rice. I usually make American fried with this dish with whole, uncooked potatoes and add a little chopped green onion to this at the end, only after potato slices are golden browned on outside and cooked through until tender on inside.

POTATO PANCAKES

3 LARGE Idaho Potatoes
2 Small onions
2 Cloves Garlic or 1 teas. Garlic Powder
Parsley & Chives from Garden
1/3 Cup Flour
2 teas. Baking Powder
1 tbs. (Heaping) Pancake Mix

Grate Potatoes by Hand or do them in blender. (I put a little in at a time so the blender doesn't stop mixing)

Add other ingredients to Grated Potatoes in blended, whirring after each ingredient.

FRY PANCAKES in vegetable oil pouring from the blender spout, (about ¼ cup).

Turn each pancake only after 1ˢᵗ side is firmed up enough to unstick to pan. Until golden brown when turned. Don't try to turn too soon or cakes will be messy and not crisp golden.

Use Non-stick Type of Fry pan & Utensils. You cannot use PAM or Vegetable Coating. You must use a good ½ cup of oil to start and add oil as it becomes deleted from pan.

Drain on plain, dry plate, not on paper towels. Grease will come off onto plate and you can then transfer pancake to another platter.

STUFFED CABBAGE/or GREEN PEPPERS

1 POUND GROUND BEEF, TURKEY OR PORK
1 COOKED AMOUNT OF 4 SERVINGS OF RICE
(Double this amount if making stuffed cabbage & peppers at same time)

½ BUNCH GREEN ONION CHOPPED
1 EGG
SALT
COURSE GROUND PEPPER
PINCH NUTMEG
PINCH ROSEMARY. THYME, MARJORAM, BASIL OR OREGANO

MIX all ingredients together while blanching cabbage leaves for at least 3 minutes in boiling water.

Fill cooled leaves with about ¼ cup amounts in inside pocket and roll. Place cabbage rolls atop filled Green Pepper cups that line bottom of large Soup pot (standing upright on their flat bottoms) after coring and filling with meat mixture. Fill Soup pot with double layer of peppers and cabbages with 1 large jar of prepared Italian Sauce or 3 cans Campbell's tomato soup (with 1 cup water added for each can), or 5 cans tomato sauce (small cans with 1 can of water added for each can).

Cook over low fire for 1 hour or until you smell the combination of the cabbage, peppers and meat. Usually about 1 hour if your soup pot holds about 6 green stuffed peppers on bottom.

COLD VALUE MEAL

TUNA WITH M ACARONI SALAD

Cook 1 package (8 oz) macaroni
SPICES & VEGGIES
1 tabls. Yellow salad mustard
1 tsp. Celery seed
1 small onion chopped
1 – 2 stalks celery finely chopped, like onion
¼ Red Onion finely chopped
1 Cup Mayonnaise (I use Lo-Fat)
½ Cup or More Ranch Style Dressing
Coarse Ground black pepper
2-3 Hard Boiled Eggs

Toss cooked macaroni after draining and rinsing with cold water with other ingredients.

Add 1 – 2 Cans Water Pack Tuna
Mix well after Tuna added

Chill in refrigerator at least one hour. The longer it is chilled, the better it tastes. It is a complete meal and is truly delicious on a hot summer's day!

GARDEN INSPIRED POOR MAN'S DISHES

VEGETABLE PANCAKES

½ Cup Flour
¼ Cup skim Milk
1 Egg, beaten
½ Baking Powder
1 cup grated carrot
1 cup grated zucchini
2 green onions, chopped

Mix together the flour, milk, egg, and baking Powder. Toss vegetables together. Stir two mixtures together. Heat a nonstick pan. Pour ¼ cup portions of pancake mixture into pan. Heat each side of each pancake 2 minutes. 4 servings.

SPAGHETTI SQUASH (OR PASTA)
WITH GARLIC AND OIL

½ Cup olive oil
6 cloves Garlic, chopped
¼ Teas. Red pepper flakes
1/3 cup water
¼ teaspoon black pepper
1//2 cup grated Parmesan Cheese

In small saucepan, heat oil over medium heat. Add garlic and pepper flakes; cook 1 minute or until garlic just starts to color; do not let garlic burn. Add water, salt and pepper. Bring to a boil.

If I have a spaghetti squash, I bake it in the oven at 30 with squash halves, cut side down, in small roasting pan. Add water. Cover pan with foil.

Bake 50-60 ninutes or until squash is fork-tender. Using fork, shred squash into strands. Place strands in large bowl. Add garlic mixture: toss. Sprinkle with Parmesan cheese.

Or cook any style of pasta according to directions. Pour garlic mixture over. Toss and serve.

When I make this next "garden" dish, I usually make enough to last 3 days, because I love it so much. I pour it over rice for a meal. And, I can eat it for 3 days without feeling whatsoever deprived. I guess the fact that I am lowering my cholesterol is another reason it turns me on. I don't let the vegetables get too mushy or it does not have the same good taste to last for a few days. Also, if the veggies stay kind of andante, the spices bring it to an even better taste in another way.

HOT OR COLD
VALUE DISH

RATATOUILLE
(French Vegetable Stew)

1 Medium sized eggplant
1 tablespoon salt
1/3 cup olive oil or vegetable oil
2 large onions, cut into rings
3 cloves garlic, crushed
2 green peppers, cut into strips
4 medium sized zucchini, cut into bite-sized pieces
2 medium, sized ripe tomatoes. Cut into wedges
14 teas. salt
Fresh ground black pepper
½ teaspoon thyme
1 bay leaf
2 table. Parsley, finely chopped

Cut eggplant into thick slices and then into small pieces. Sprinkle with salt. Allow eggplant to stand for 30 minutes, then rinse and pat dry on paper towels. Heat the oil in a large skillet. Sauté onions and green pepper and cook for two minutes,. Add eggplant and cook stirring constantly. Add zucchini and continue stirring for three minutes. Add tomatoes, salt, pepper, thyme and bay leaf. Simmer uncovered for 30 minutes until all the vegetables are tender. Remove bay leaf. Garnish with parsley and serve hot. Ratatouille can also be served cold as an appetizer to scoop with crackers or cucumber slices, or pour over rice pasta or mashed potatoes.

CANNED SOUP ENTREES

Using soup for a meal is easy and tasty if you use textures of soups with accompaniments of starches that you enjoy.

CREAM OF MUSHROOM SOUP is delicious over wide egg noodles. It tastes like Beef Stroganoff.

HEARTY BEEF WITH VEGETABLE is great over rice. It tastes like a Beef Stew over rice.

When my daughter lived in Washington, D.C. (her first job away from home) she lived on combinations like this for five years. She had the lowest cholesterol of anyone I ever knew, even at her age, and she was as thin as a pencil.

PERFECT EVERY TIME MEATLOAF

3-4 lbs. Ground Beef (4th lb. May be added as Ground Pork)
1 Package Dry Onion Soup Mix
1 –2 Eggs
Garlic Salt, pinches
Black Coarse Ground Pepper, pinches
Seasoned Salt ½ Teaspoon
¼ Cup Worcestershire Sauce
3 Tabls. Parsley
3 Tabls. Basil, or Oregano
½ Cup Parmesan Cheese
1 Cup Italian Bread Crumbs

Mix all ingredients in any order until meat and seasonings are evenly mixed.

Form narrow Meat Load and lay out on shallow baking pan. NOT MEAT LOAF PAN. (FAT STAYS IN MEAT LOAD PAN AND MEAT LOAF DOES NOT COOK RIGHT IN THIS WAY) Use of shallow baking pan will make it taste like a roast!

Roast @ 350 45 minutes or until smells like Meat Loaf.

OLGA'S BAKED BABY LIMAS

2 Tabls. Karo Syrup (Dark, if possible, but light OK)
Fry 1 onion in ¼ stick butter
1 Can Tomato Soup
Baby Lima Beans cooked for 30 minutes

Combine above ingredients and bake 350 for 30 – 40 minutes.

Just pick a variety of soup you like and pair it with something good to pour it over. I especially like Cream of Asparagus over Scrambled eggs because I try to avoid carbohydrates as much I can.

AUTUMN PEASANT STEW

ANY KIND OF PORK DERIVATIVE OF MEAT
KIELBASA (POLISH OR ANY TYPE SAUSAGE, KNOCK OR BRAT)
HOT DOGS OR ANY LEFT OVER SMOKED BUTT TYPE MEATS
PORK SHOULDER CHOPS
SPARE RIBS OR PORK SHANKS
1 LARGE CAN OR JAR SAUERKRAUT (Fresh cabbage also can be used)
4 POTATOES QUARTERED (Add 2 tables. vinegar)
1-2 LARGE TOMATOES—WEDGES
1 LARGE APPLE—EIGHTHED
1 LARGE ONION—QUARTERED
½ Green Pepper, if I have it, chopped
1 TABLS. CARRAWAY SEED
2 TABLS. BROWN SUGAR

Everything can be put into electric frypan or slowcooker, or Dutch oven without other preparation, unless you are using Pork Shoulder chops or Spare Ribs OR Pork Shanks. These last 3 taste better and give the dish a better porky, meaty flavor if they are browned first. I prefer to use an electric fry pan and brown my meat first and then add all the other ingredients, adding the sauerkraut first, then adding the seasonings and stirring. Then add the vegetables and 1 cup water and cook until meat is tender and flavors smell melded together.

If I use Hot Dogs I slice them on a diagonal and then cooking time is a lot less than using Meat that takes time to cook. If I have a long Polish type sausage, I also slice this in diagonals. Cooking time for Hot Dogs and Sausages can be only about 30 minutes whereas meat in this dish, takes about 2 hours to cook. Occasionally you will have to stir and add more water and check the cooking.

Whatever you contribute, it's delicious, no one is unhappy and CAN TAKE seconds. The combinations of textures and flavors of kraut and meat and sweet & sour and is scrumptious for copper pennies and sustains all year. So much so, that, like my family, no one complains when it is made with just Franks. They PREFER it the Dogger way!

This dish is special because it actually has the flavor of Autumn all year!

CHAPTER ELEVEN

PASTELES & POSTRIES

Like desserts, this chapter is short and dulce! Only the best of what I have learned to create over the years is represented here. The best entertainment recipes, and those that my family most frequently requested.

My favorite holiday is Easter. I bake a lot to announce the onset of the Spring season and because I simply have more time to do so than at Christmas.

The following are lusciously SUPERIOR, SIMPLE and EXQUISITE.

BEST CHEESECAKE

5-8 oz. Cream cheese
1 cup sugar
1 & 1/3 Tabls. Argo Cornstarch
5 large eggs
1 tabls. vanilla
¼ cup whipping cream
½ cup Sour cream

Blend cream cheese, sugar and cornstarch together. Add eggs one at a time. Add vanilla whipping cream and sour cream.

(For chocolate cheesecake add 4 oz. Ghiradellii bittersweet chocolate, melted and cooled before you blend into cheesecake mixture.)

CRUST

1 ½ packages graham crackers – crushed
½ cup sugar
Handful coconut
Stick of butter melted

Blend dry ingredients; add melted butter and put in bottom of greased springform pan (uses Pam butter spray on bottom and sides).

Pour cheesecake mixture over crust. Wrap springform pan with heavy tin foil near to the top. Place on cookie sheet (with sides). Pour water onto cookie sheet to near top of edge. (Considered a "baking water bath!, prevents cheesecake from cracking; may be a little water left even though cake is done.)

Bake at 350 degrees for 1 hour and approx. 10-15 minutes; Check after 1 hour. Should be a light golden on top. Check edge with toothpick, middle will shake.

Cool approximately 2 hours in pan, or until cake pulls away from sides.

Unmask (remove side of spring form), refrigerate a t least 8 hours before cutting.

Remove bottom of pan before freezing if your are considering freezing whole or in sections. Freezes well up to 6 months.

You can make Sour Cream topping if you wish with:

12 tsp. Almond extract
1 ½ cup sour cream
½ tsp. Vanilla Mix together and frost top of cheesecake after cool & set in fridge at least 1 more hour.

NEW YORK CHEESECAKE

(BANISH BELLY FAT)
8 OZ. LIT CREAM CHEESE
1 CUP LOW-FAT RICOTTA
2 EGGS SEPARATED
¼ CUP HONEY
¼ CUP Gold raisins
3—Tabls. Cornstarch
1 Tabls. Grated orange rind (now called orange zest)
1/3 cup amaretto cookie crumbs (Can mix ½ cup Amaretto into crumbs)

Preheat oven to 400. Combine cream cheese, & ricotta until smooth. Stir in egg yolks, honey, raisins, cornstarch and orange rind, mix till combined well.

Mix egg white with clean beaters 2 minute or until form stiff peaks. Fold white into cheese mixture.

Coat 9" pie pan with nonstick spray and cover with Amaretto crumbs.

Pour cheese mixture into pie plats. Bake 30 mins. Or until golden and set.
12 Servings
121 Calories
5.2 Grams Fat

1-2-3-4—MEASURE CAKE

(Old family treasure)
3 cups sifted flour
3 Teas. Baking powder
¼ Teas. Salt
1 cup shortening
2 cups sugar
1 Teas. Vanilla
4 eggs separated
1 cup milk

Sift flour, baking powder & salt together. Cream shortening, with sugar and vanilla until fluffy. Add beaten egg yolks & beat thoroughly. Add sifted dry ingredients and milk alternately in small amounts beating well after each addition. Beat egg whites until stiff but not dry and fold into batter. Pour into 3 greased 9 inch pans and bake 30 mins. At 375.

LEMON WONDER CAKE

1 Lemon Cake Mix BUNDT PAN
2 4 Eggs
3 1 pkg. Lemon Jell-O
4 ¾ Cup oil

Mix Jell-O with 1 cup hot water to dissolve – put aside to cool. Mix Cake mix with oil and eggs, mixing after each egg. Add cooled Jell-O & pour into greased tube pan. Bake 350 for 40 ins. Dribble orange icing on warm cake, poking holes with fork to absorb icing.

(You can also make a chocolate version of this cake by using a Duncan Hines Chocolate cake mix and piercing holes in the warm cake and then pouring chocolate syrup over the cake while still warm, so that chocolate drips down into cake.)

CRÈME BRULEE

BAKED CUSTARD RECIPE
3 SLIGHTLY BEATEN EGGS
¼ CUP SUGAR
¼ TESAS. SALT
2 CUPS MILK, SCALDED
½ TO 1 TEAS. VANILLA

DO ABOVE BAKED CUSTARD RECIPE, EXCEPT FOR VANILLA

Combine eggs, sugar and salt.

Slowly stir in slightly cooled milk and vanilla

Set six 5 oz custard cups in shallow pan on oven rack. Pour hot water around them. 1 inch rack. Pour in custard.

Bake in slow oven (325) 40 TO 45 MINUTES OR OOUNTIL KNIFE INSERTED OFF-CENTER COMES OUT CLEAN. Serve warm, or chilled. To unsalted chilled cup custard, first loosen edge; then skip point of knife, down side, to let air in. Insert

For one large custard, bake in quart casserole about 60 minutes till done.

YOU MAY USE PACKAGED CUSTARD INSTEAD OF ABOVE PROCESS.

Prepare custard as above using light cream or whipping cream instead of milk, cooking custard 2 minutes after it coats spoon.

Cool, pour into 8 inch round baking dish.

Sift ½ cup brown sugar over custard. Set in shallow pan; surround with ice cubes in a little cold water. Broil 8 inches from heat about 5 minutes. Till custard has bubbly brown crust. Serve immediately; or chill. Serve over fruit or trim with fruit as is.

GERTIE'S CREPE SUZETTES

9 Servings / 18 Crepes

Batter:

1 ¼ Cup Milk
1 Egg
1 Egg yolk
1 tabls. butter melted
1/3 teaspoon salt
2 Tabls. sugar
1 Cup sifted flour
1 Tabls. vegetable oil

Sauce:

3 Tabls. butter
3 tabls sugar
Rind of one orange
Juice of two oranges
2 Tabls. Grand Mariner or other orange liqueur

Place milk, egg, egg yolk, butter, salt, sugar and flavor, in a blender. Blend one minute until smooth. Oil frying pan and prepare crepes following the directions below.

That is, pour in a spoonful of batter. Rotate pan in all directions to coat the surface with batter evenly. (As in an omelet) Tip out any excess batter. Cook one minute until crepe is lightly browned. Turn and brown on the second side. (Discard the first crepe which will be oily), Place a teaspoon of butter and honey on each crepe, (au meil) style or a teaspoon of apple butter. Fold and serve hot. I fill with prune butter or apple butter. Years ago we called it povidla and we were able to buy it fresh in a deli. Now, it is a little hard to find in a jar, but you can use any kind of preserves you prefer to roll it up with after covering the thin crepe with the substance evenly and thinly.

TO GERTIE, MY MOTHER.....
MY FIRST COOKING TEACHER

THAT'S ALL
FOLKS!

COOK AND ENJOY!

INDEX